SURVIVING WITH RICE AND BEANS COOKBOOK

DISCOVER HOW TO THRIVE DURING ANY EMERGENCY
WITH THIS COMPLETE COOKBOOK.
1000 DAYS OF EASY-TO-REPLICATE, NUTRIENT-DENSE,
AND TASTY RICE & BEANS RECIPES

EVINNAH COUD

COPYRIGHT

TABLE OF CONTENTS

CHAPTER 4
DAILY RICE RECIPES 61

INTRODUCTION

Because beans contain lectins or proteins that make them difficult to digest, they must be soaked before cooking. Soaking them overnight in plenty of water is a simple way to get rid of these proteins. You should also remove the hulls before boiling them for about 5 hours because they are difficult to digest as well. The longer you cook the beans, the better your meal will be.

Rice is another food that can be prepared in an emergency because it is widely available and simple to prepare. It must, however, be kept dry because it tends to stick together when wet. It is critical to clean the rice before cooking by washing away impurities and soaking it overnight to achieve a better texture in the final dish. You can boil or steam your rice, but I prefer to do both in a pressure cooker to save time.

Beans are also high in fiber, which helps to slow digestion. This means you can avoid hunger for a longer period. Beans also help to maintain a healthy digestive tract and lower the chances of constipation. Rice, on the other hand, is a carbohydrate that provides energy. It also contains a significant amount of methionine, an essential amino acid that beans lack.

Airtight containers should not be used to keep rice. Airtight containers can become hot, causing the rice to sweat. If the rice begins to sweat, it creates a haven for mold. The beauty of rice is that it is inexpensive to store. Simply purchase a regular food-grade container and ensure that it is properly secured.

Beans and rice are both fantastic staple goods to establish a stockpile in your house. They taste wonderful, are simple to cook, and are high in protein. They can offer you the necessary nutrition, but they cannot provide you with all of your vital vitamins and minerals.

This book focuses on the importance of beans in survival food because they can make any meal more satisfying without requiring too much time cooking or searching for ingredients that may not be available during an emergency. This Cookbook also will teach you how to transform simple beans and rice into tasty, morale-boosting meals, snacks, drinks, desserts, and more.

CHAPTER 1
ORIGINS OF RICE AND BEANS

Black beans, along with other varieties of dry beans, are a staple food in many Latin American and other civilizations around the world. Beans, in one form or another, are included in nearly every meal in Latin America and the Caribbean. They, especially dried beans, are a fantastic low-cost protein source and can be stored for quite some time.

Types of Rice

Long-grain rice has a long, slender kernel that is 4-5 times as long as it is wide. When grains are cooked, they become distinct, light, and fluffy. When opposed to Indian basmati rice, which cooks to separate grains that are drier and fluffier, Thai jasmine rice is moister and clings together. When cooked, basmati rice retains its characteristic shape and is perfect for curries and stews.

The kernel of medium-grain rice is shorter and wider than that of long-grain rice. Cooked grains are moister and soft, and they cling together more than long grain grains. Arborio rice is a short to medium grain Italian rice that is commonly used in risotto and paella dishes. Such grains absorb cooking liquid while remaining thick and distinct in shape.

Short-grain rice has a short, plump kernel that is virtually spherical. Cooked grains are mushy and adhere to one another. This type of sticky rice is a staple in Japan and Korea. It is also often used to make sushi rice because the starch released generates the stickiness required for sushi rolls.

Types of Beans

Most supermarkets and grocery stores will stock a wide variety of beans and legumes, both in dried form and canned. This chapter has a simple list of the most common beans and legumes that you will come across.

So, experiment with the different options open to you and see what you like best:

- Chickpeas
- Edamame
- Lentils
- Lima Beans
- Kidney Beans
- Adzuki Beans
- Black Beans
- Black Eyed Peas

Preparation and Cooking

Beans come canned or dried. But, what is the difference between them? Well, there is no nutritional difference between canned or dried, the main difference comes down to preparation. Canned beans and legumes are great when you're in a rush, just pop a can open, rinse in a fine-mesh sieve, and drain.

Dried beans and legumes take a lot longer to cook, plus they need to be pre-soaked. I find that they are slightly tastier, but not by much.

So, it comes down to your preference and how much time you have to spare.

If you choose to go the dried route, which many of the recipes in this book call for, you will need to soak your beans or legumes first.

The best way to do this is to add your dried beans or legumes to a pot and cover them with water. Cover the pot and leave for 8+ hours, but ideally, leave overnight. Drain them off in a sieve and rinse well.

When it comes to cooking, it is a good idea to make large batches ahead of time, as they will keep for around 5 days in the refrigerator.

How to Cook?

1. Add the beans or legumes to a pot and cover it with water.
2. Place over high heat and bring to a boil. Once boiling, reduce the heat to low, stir, and cover.
3. Let the pot simmer for anywhere between 30-45 minutes, stirring occasionally.
4. Remove the cover 5 minutes before finished cooking time. Optional: Season with sea salt and ground black pepper; stir to mix.
5. If there is any water remaining in the pot, then drain it off in a fine-mesh sieve. If more water is required during the cooking process add ½ cup at a time. Follow the below section on "tips of cooking" for further information to make sure your dried beans and legumes cook perfectly every time.

Tips on Cooking

- Aim for around 3 times the amount of water for beans and legumes.
- Add garlic, spices, and herbs of your choice when cooking, add to the water, and stir well.
- 1 pound of dried beans/legumes will yield around 5-6 cups of the cooked product.
- You know they are properly cooked when you can easily mush one between your finger and thumb with only a little pressure.
- Don't add salt, or anything acidic, to the pot until almost finished cooking, as it can dry the beans out if added too early.

Benefits of Beans

- **Beans play a vital role** in improving our holistic health by optimally nourishing our bodies from within. Let's take a glance at the nutritional capabilities of these superfoods.
- **Protein**: Beans are a rich source of plant-based protein that is easy for the body to digest. For vegans and vegetarians; they are an excellent source of protein to compensate for the meat-derived protein.
- **Antioxidants**: Apart from protein, beans also provide antioxidants in spades. Antioxidants help to fight off harmful effects caused by free radicals. Excessive amounts of free radicals can damage metabolic functions and lead to the development of many critical health diseases.
- **Fiber and Mineral Boost**: Being a rich source of dietary fibers, beans help improve digestive functions and keep digestive disorders at bay. In people with diabetes, increased fiber consumption can lower their glucose levels.
- **A fiber-rich diet also increases satiety**, leading to reduced food intake and helping prevent unwanted weight gain.
- **Beans are also rich** in potassium, iron, zinc, and magnesium to ensure the healthy functioning of the brain, heart, bones, and muscles.
- **Improved Heart Health**: Beans are very well-known foods for improving heart health. They reduce the level of bad cholesterol in the body to decrease the risk of heart attack and other cardiovascular conditions.
- **Decreased Disease Factor**: By providing essential nutrients, including more beans in our diet reduces the development of harmful diseases and conditions, including diabetes, obesity, and many types of cancer.

Rice Cooking Tips

- Before adding the rice, always bring the water to a boil. It is critical to cook rice in a saucepan with a lid. The rice will absorb the water and cook evenly as a result. You can cook rice without a lid on the pan, but the recipe will require more water and the cooking time may be longer. If cooked in this manner, the rice may become mushier. Cook only until the rice is tender; otherwise, the rice will become gummy.

- When making rice for a savory dish or rice bowls, I always cook it in vegetable or chicken broth and add onion and garlic to the rice as it cooks for added flavor. To achieve different flavors, try cooking the rice in wine, beer, or fruit juice. To add to rice, keep the dried minced onion and jarred minced garlic on hand.

- When cooking rice, add a few drops of Tabasco sauce to the boiling water to enhance the flavor. Adding 2 teaspoons of vinegar to the boiling water can also improve the flavor of the rice. You can also substitute fresh lemon juice for the vinegar.

- After the rice comes to a boil, do not stir it. It will gummy the rice.

- Cooked rice will keep in the refrigerator for about 5 days. Cooked rice can be frozen for 3 months. When rice is frozen, it is easier to use in recipes. I freeze rice in 1-cup increments. If you are using frozen rice in a casserole or main dish, you do not need to thaw it.

- To reheat leftover rice, add 2 teaspoons of water to each cup. Microwave or heat the rice in a pot. Heat the rice in a small saucepan over low heat until it is hot and fluffy.

- Cooked rice should not be left in the pan for longer than 10 minutes. The rice begins to cool and gel. This results in extremely bland rice. Remember that leftover rice can be used to thicken soups instead of flour or cornstarch. Some people believe that rice is bland and requires a lot of flavors, so be generous with the herbs and spices.

CHAPTER 2
SURVIVAL RICE RECIPES

1. SIMPLE RED BEANS AND RICE

Preparation Time: 7 minutes   **Cooking Time:** 2 hours   **Servings:** 6-8

INGREDIENTS

- 2 ½ cups cooked rice
- 1 pound dried red beans
- 6 cups vegetable broth
- 1 medium yellow onion, finely chopped
- 4 garlic cloves, minced
- 4 stalks celery, finely chopped
- Bunch green onions, sliced
- 1 medium bell pepper, finely chopped
- 2 tablespoons olive oil
- 1 teaspoon oregano
- 1 teaspoon thyme
- ½ tablespoon smoked paprika
- 1 whole bay leaf
- Pinch cayenne pepper
- Pinch freshly cracked pepper

DIRECTIONS

1. Place the beans in a large pot and fill it with cool water. Place in the fridge to soak overnight.
2. Heat the olive oil in a large pot over medium heat and add the chopped onion, bell pepper, celery, and garlic. Sauté for about 5-7 minutes, until the vegetables have softened.
3. Drain the beans and rinse with cool water. Add the beans to the pot with vegetables and stir well.
4. Pour in the vegetable broth and add all the spices. Cover the pot and bring it to a boil. Turn the heat down and leave it to simmer for at least 2 hours. Stir occasionally to prevent the vegetables from sticking to the bottom.
5. When the beans are tender and soft, use a fork or the back of a spoon to mash some of the beans against the side of the pot.
6. Remove the bay leaf and let it simmer for about 30 minutes more until the mixture thickens a bit.
7. Serve immediately. Divide the beans into bowls and top with a scoop of warm, cooked rice. Sprinkle with sliced green onions.

Nutrition: Calories: 1086; Protein 46 g; Carbohydrates 147 g; Fat 29 g; Sodium 225 mg

2. SLOW COOKER BEANS AND RICE GUMBO

Preparation Time: 8 minutes   **Cooking Time:** 25 minutes   **Servings:** 4-6

INGREDIENTS

For Beans and Rice:
- 1 ½ cup canned kidney beans, rinsed and drained
- 1 ¾ cup canned diced tomatoes
- 8 ounces white mushrooms, quartered
- 1 ½ cup rice
- 1 cup frozen sliced okra
- 1 small zucchini, thickly cut
- 2 cups vegetable broth
- 3 garlic cloves, minced
- 1 bay leaf
- 2 stalks celery, chopped
- 1 green bell pepper, chopped
- 1 yellow onion, chopped
- 2 tablespoons olive oil, divided
- 2 tablespoons all-purpose flour
- 1 tablespoon cajun seasoning
- 2 tablespoons vegan Worcestershire sauce
- Salt and pepper to taste

For Vegan Worcestershire Sauce:
- 1 cup apple cider vinegar
- 1/8 cup light brown sugar
- ¼ cup soy sauce
- ½ garlic clove, crushed
- ½ teaspoon dry mustard
- ½ teaspoon ground ginger
- ½ teaspoon onion powder
- ¼ teaspoon freshly ground black pepper
- ¼ teaspoon ground cinnamon

DIRECTIONS

For Vegan Worcestershire Sauce:
1. In a medium saucepan, add all the ingredients and bring to a boil. Turn down the heat and leave it to simmer for about 20 minutes. When the liquid is reduced by half, remove it from the heat and strain through a sieve. Leave the sauce to cool completely before using it. Store in an airtight container and keep it in the fridge.

For Beans and Rice:
2. In a Dutch oven, heat 1 tablespoon of olive oil over medium heat. Add the bell pepper, onion, garlic, and celery; cook for about 8-10 minutes, until softened. Transfer to a 4-6-quart slow cooker.
3. Return the Dutch oven to the stove and heat the remaining tablespoon of olive oil. Stir in the flour and cook, stirring for about 4 minutes, until it becomes golden brown. Add the vegetable broth and bring it to a boil. Transfer the mixture to the slow cooker.
4. Place all the remaining ingredients into the slow cooker, except the rice. Cover the slow cooker and cook for about 6-8 hours. When done, remove the bay leaf, check the flavors, and season with salt and pepper if needed.
5. Place the rice in a saucepan filled with water and bring it to a boil. Reduce the heat and simmer until tender.
6. Serve warm over hot steaming rice.

Nutrition: Calories: 754; Protein 26 g; Carbohydrates 102 g; Fat 29 g; Sodium 189 mg

3. CURRIED LENTILS AND RICE

Preparation Time: 8 minutes   **Cooking Time:** 35 minutes   **Servings:** 4

INGREDIENTS

- 1 pound uncooked lentils, rinsed and soaked (if desired)
- 8 cups water, more as needed
- 3 ½ quarts (14 cups) vegetable or chicken broth, divided
- 3/4 cup diced dehydrated onions
- 1 ½ cup freeze-dried carrot cubes
- 2 (15 ounces) cans petite diced tomatoes, undrained
- 1 ½ teaspoon dehydrated minced garlic
- 1 teaspoon salt, more to taste
- 1 ½ cup canned evaporated milk (or 3/4 cup powdered milk mixed with 1 ½ cup water)
- 1/3 cup sour cream powder
- 1 tablespoon curry powder, more to taste
- 1 cup hot cooked rice

DIRECTIONS

1. Add the lentils, water, and 6 cups broth to a large stock pot (liquid should just cover beans). Bring to a boil, then lower heat to medium. Simmer for 35 minutes or 1 hour, adding more liquid if needed. Add the rest of the broth (8 cups or 2 quarts), vegetables, garlic, and curry; stir well. Cook until vegetables are tender and the liquid is reduced. Before serving, add milk and sour cream powder; mix well using a whisk. Add more curry and salt as desired.
2. Serve over hot and cooked rice.

Nutrition: Calories: 1707; Protein 146 g; Carbohydrates 119 g; Fat 20 g; Sodium 560 mg

4. BLACK BEAN BURGERS

Preparation Time: 8 minutes   **Cooking Time:** 60 minutes   **Servings:** 4

INGREDIENTS

- 2 (15 ounces) cans black beans, drained
- 1/4 cup freeze-dried green peppers, reconstituted
- 1/2 cup breadcrumbs or oats
- 1/2 teaspoon onion powder
- 1 fresh egg or 1 flax egg*
- 1/2 teaspoon garlic powder
- 1/4 teaspoon chili powder
- 1/2 teaspoon cumin
- 1/4 teaspoon ground black pepper
- Salt to taste
- Oil, as required
- Freeze-dried shredded cheese, reconstituted (optional)

DIRECTIONS

1. Reconstitute peppers and cheese (if using) in separate bowls.
2. In a medium-sized bowl, mash black beans where they are still a little chunky. Add all of the remaining ingredients except oil and cheese, and mix well with your hands. Form into 4-5 patties. Heat oil in a pan (or grease the grill if using). Fry or grill just like you would a beef burger.
3. If desired, top patties with your choice of cheese, reduce heat to low, and cover with a lid to melt the cheese.
4. You may also top with gravy if available. Serve with vegetables and/or rice.

* Flax egg: Mix 1 tablespoon of ground flax and 3 tablespoons of warm water in a small bowl. Set aside for at least 5 minutes before using.
Note: Mayonnaise is also a good egg substitute if you don't have fresh eggs. Just use 1 heaped spoonful for each egg needed.

Nutrition: Calories: 716; Protein 46 g; Carbohydrates 106 g; Fat 14 g; Sodium 530 mg

5. TOMATO RICE AND BEANS

Preparation Time: 7 minutes   **Cooking Time:** 25 minutes   **Servings:** 6-8

INGREDIENTS

- 1-2 cups medium-grain white rice
- 1 ½ cup canned black beans, drained and rinsed
- 1 ½ cup canned tomatoes, diced
- ¼ cup finely chopped fresh cilantro leaves
- ¼ cup finely chopped fresh oregano leaves
- 6 medium garlic cloves, finely chopped
- 1 medium fresh jalapeno, cored, finely chopped
- 2 tablespoons extra-virgin olive oil
- 2 teaspoons ground cumin
- 2 tablespoons kosher or fine sea salt
- 1 teaspoon chili powder

DIRECTIONS

1. Combine the rice with 2 cups of cold water in a saucepan. When it starts boiling, cover the pot, reduce the heat and let it simmer for 20 minutes. When done, remove from the heat and let it stand covered for about 5 minutes.
2. Set a fine sieve in a bowl; pour the canned tomatoes and drain. Pour the tomato juices into a cup (reserving the tomatoes) and pour in enough water to equal 1 cup.
3. Heat a large skillet over medium-high heat. Add the oil, jalapeno, and garlic; sauté, stirring frequently for about 1 minute, until the garlic browns. Stir in the beans and spices and cook for 1 minute more. Pour in the tomato and water mixture and bring to a boil. Cook for about 5-7 minutes, stirring occasionally, until the beans have absorbed most of the liquid.
4. Add the oregano and cilantro leaves, tomatoes, and cooked rice. Cook for 1-2 minutes, stirring occasionally.
5. Serve immediately.

Nutrition: Calories: 346; Protein 55 g; Carbohydrates 183 g; Fat 25 g; Sodium 145 mg

6. INDIAN RICE AND BEANS

Preparation Time: 7 minutes   **Cooking Time:** 55 minutes   **Servings:** 4

INGREDIENTS

- 1 ½ cup (or 1 can) canned kidney beans, drained and rinsed
- 2 cups vegetable broth
- 1 cup unsweetened coconut milk
- 1 cup thinly sliced green onions
- ¾ cup medium-grain white rice
- 1 jalapeno, deseeded and minced
- ½ teaspoon ground allspice
- 1 teaspoon dried thyme

DIRECTIONS

1. Combine all the ingredients, except the green onion and rice, in a medium or large saucepan. Bring to a boil and add the rice. Reduce the heat and let the mixture simmer for about 20 minutes, until the liquid has been absorbed and the rice is tender.
2. Stir in some of the green onions, using the rest for the garnish. Cook until the rice is completely tender.
3. Serve immediately with the remaining green onions.

Nutrition: Calories: 585; Protein 25.3 g; Carbohydrates 124 g; Fat 19 g; Sodium 480 mg

7. CHICKPEAS BEAN AND RICE

Preparation Time: 7 minutes   **Cooking Time:** 43 minutes   **Servings:** 4

INGREDIENTS

- 2 cups rice
- ½ cup red kidney beans
- ½ cup garbanzo beans (chickpeas), drained and rinsed
- ½ cup black beans, drained and rinsed
- ¾ cups diced tomatoes
- 1 large green bell pepper, seeded and chopped
- 1 large red onion, peeled and chopped
- 1 tablespoon olive oil
- 2 teaspoons minced garlic
- 1 tablespoon curry powder
- 3 tablespoons peanut butter
- 1 teaspoon ground ginger
- 1 teaspoon ground cumin

DIRECTIONS

1. Prepare the rice according to the package directions.
2. In the meantime, heat the oil in a deep skillet over medium heat. Add the chopped onion and sauté for a few minutes, until softened. Add the chopped bell pepper and sauté for 2-3 minutes. Stir in the minced garlic and cook for 1 more minute, stirring frequently.
3. Pour in the kidney beans with the juices and the tomatoes, then stir well to combine the ingredients. Cook for about 5 minutes, stirring occasionally.
4. Add the ginger, cumin, curry powder, and peanut butter, stirring gently so as not to break up the beans. When the peanut butter is well blended with the rest of the ingredients, add the drained garbanzo and black beans. Stir well.
5. Reduce the heat to low and simmer uncovered, until the mixture thickens a bit.
6. When the rice is done, divide into bowls and top it with the beans stew.

Nutrition: Calories: 967; Protein 35 g; Carbohydrates 154 g; Fat 27 g; Sodium 202 mg

8. BLACK BEANS AND COCONUT RICE

Preparation Time: 7 minutes   **Cooking Time:** 43 minutes   **Servings:** 4

INGREDIENTS

For Beans and Rice:
- 1 cup rice
- 1 cup unsweetened flaked coconut
- 3 ½-4 cups vegetable broth, divided
- ¾ cup chopped fresh cilantro
- 3 cups (or 2 cans) canned black beans, drained and rinsed
- ½ large onion, chopped
- 3 green onions, sliced
- 1 lime
- ¼ teaspoon pepper
- ¼ teaspoon salt
- 4 tablespoons coconut oil, divided
- ¼ teaspoon cayenne pepper
- 2 teaspoons chili powder

For Mango Salsa:
- 2 ripe mangos, chopped
- Bunch cilantro, stems removed, chopped
- 1 lime, juiced
- 1 red onion, chopped

DIRECTIONS

For Mango Salsa:
1. In a medium bowl, combine all the ingredients. Mix well and place in the fridge for about 1 hour.

For Beans and Rice:
2. Preheat oven to 350°F. Spread the coconut on a baking sheet and toast it for about 5-10 minutes.
3. In a large saucepan, pour 2 ½ cups of the vegetable broth, add 2 tablespoons of coconut oil and season with salt and pepper and bring to a boil. Add the rice, cover the pot, reduce the heat to low, and simmer for 20 minutes, or until the liquid has been absorbed.
4. Heat the remaining coconut oil in a large skillet over medium heat. Add the onions and sauté for about 5-7 minutes. Add the black beans, 1 cup of vegetable broth, and spices. Cook for about 15 minutes, stirring occasionally. If the mixture appears to be too dry, pour in a little more broth. When done, remove from the heat.
5. To prepare the lime, roll it out on the counter to loosen the juices, pressing with your palm as you roll. Cut the lime in half and squeeze the juice into the pot with beans. Add the toasted coconut and chopped cilantro. Stir well to combine.
6. When serving, spoon the rice onto a plate and top it with the beans and the mango salsa.

Nutrition: Calories: 864; Protein 27 g; Carbohydrates 134 g; Fat 35 g; Sodium 800 mg; Sugar 1 g

9. CURRY RICE AND LENTILS

Preparation Time: 7 minutes   **Cooking Time:** 55 minutes   **Servings:** 4

INGREDIENTS

- ½ cup basmati rice
- 1 cup brown lentils, soaked, rinsed, and drained
- 3 cups water
- 1 cup diced tomato
- 1 cup frozen peas, defrosted
- 1 ½ cup chopped onions
- 2 garlic cloves, minced
- 1 small hot pepper, minced
- 2 teaspoons canola oil
- 1 teaspoon ginger, minced
- ½-1 teaspoon salt
- 1 tablespoon curry powder
- 3-4 tablespoons chopped cilantro, for garnish

DIRECTIONS

1. Heat the oil in a medium-size saucepan over medium heat. Add the chopped onions, ginger, pepper, and garlic. Sauté for about 1-2 minutes.
2. When the onions begin to soften, add the rice, lentils, and curry powder, then pour in water. Stir well, cover the pan and bring to a boil. Reduce the heat and simmer for about 35 minutes.
3. Remove the pot from the heat, add the peas, cover the pot again and let it sit for 5 minutes.
4. Stir in the tomatoes, season with salt, and fluff with a fork.
5. Serve immediately with some chopped cilantro on top.

Nutrition: Calories: 686; Protein 43 g; Carbohydrates 96 g; Fat 16 g; Sodium 950 mg; Sugar 0 g

10. DOMINICAN RICE AND BEANS

Preparation Time: 7 minutes   **Cooking Time:** 32 minutes   **Servings:** 6

INGREDIENTS

- 4 cups rice
- 6 cups water
- 2 cups canned kidney beans
- ¼ cup chopped cubanelle peppers
- ¼ cup chopped celery
- 1/8 cup sliced pitted olives (optional)
- 1/8 cup capers (optional)
- 2 tablespoons tomato paste
- 5 tablespoons oil, divided
- ½ teaspoon mashed garlic
- ½ teaspoon dry thyme leaves
- 1 teaspoon finely chopped fresh cilantro
- 1 teaspoon salt
- Pinch oregano

DIRECTIONS

1. Heat half the amount of oil over high heat in an iron pot. Add the garlic, celery, coriander, oregano, thyme, capers, and peppers. Stir in the tomato paste until the tomato dissolves.
2. Add the beans, stir well, and season with salt.
3. Pour in the water and bring to a boil. Taste to check for salt, if needed, add some more salt, bearing in mind that rice will absorb most of the salt. Add the rice, stirring occasionally so as not to allow the rice to stick to the bottom.
4. When the water has evaporated, cover the pan and simmer for about 15 minutes. Add the remaining oil and stir well. Continue simmering for another 5 minutes. If the rice looks too dry, pour in about ¼ cup of boiling water and continue simmering. When the rice is tender, remove from the heat.
5. Serve warm.

Nutrition: Calories: 1673; Protein 33 g; Carbohydrates 221 g; Fat 78 g; Sodium 209 mg

11. EASTERN RICE AND BEANS

Preparation Time: 7 minutes   **Cooking Time:** 43 minutes   **Servings:** 4

INGREDIENTS

- 1 ½ cup black beans, drained and rinsed
- 1 ½ cup chickpeas (garbanzo beans), drained and rinsed
- 1 cup white rice
- 2 ½ cups vegetable broth
- 1 garlic clove, minced
- 1 tablespoon olive oil
- 1/8 teaspoon ground cayenne pepper
- 2 teaspoons ground coriander
- 2 teaspoons ground cumin
- ½ teaspoon curry powder
- 1 teaspoon ground turmeric
- Pepper and salt to taste
- Naan or flatbread, as required

DIRECTIONS

1. Heat the olive oil in a large skillet over medium heat. Add the garlic and sauté for 1 minute. Add the rice, stir well and add all the spices. Cook for about 5 minutes.
2. Pour in the vegetable broth and bring it to a boil. Reduce the heat, cover the skillet and let the mixture simmer for 20 minutes.
3. Add the black beans and garbanzo beans. Stir gently.
4. Serve warm over flat bread or naan.

Nutrition: Calories: 986; Protein: 43 g; Carbohydrates: 127 g; Fat: 34 g; Sugar: 0.9 g;Sodium: 730 mg

12. SPANISH-STYLE BLACK BEANS AND RICE

Preparation Time: 7 minutes   **Cooking Time:** 33 minutes   **Servings:** 8

INGREDIENTS

- ½ cup brown rice
- ½ cup canned black beans, drained and rinsed well
- 1 ½ cup diced tomatoes, fresh or canned
- 1 yellow pepper, stemmed, deseeded, chopped
- 1 medium onion, chopped
- 2 garlic cloves, minced
- ½ jalapeno chilies, stemmed, deseeded, finely diced
- 1 teaspoon ancho powder
- 1 teaspoon ground cumin
- ½ teaspoon smoked paprika
- ½ teaspoon chili powder
- Pepper and salt to taste

DIRECTIONS

1. Place the rice in a saucepan filled with water and bring it to a boil. Reduce the heat and simmer until tender.
2. Heat a deep skillet over medium-high heat. Add the onion and cook, stirring until it begins to brown. Stir in the garlic, jalapeno, and pepper and cook for about 2 minutes, paying attention not to burn the garlic.
3. Add the rest of the ingredients along with the cooked rice and cook for 15 minutes more, stirring frequently. If it appears to be dry, pour in a little reserved tomato juice or vegetable broth.
4. Check the flavor, adjust the seasonings if necessary, and serve warm.

Nutrition: Calories: 248; Protein 9 g; Carbohydrates 50 g; Fat 7.6 g; Sugar 9 g; Sodium 590 mg

13. TASTY RICE AND BEANS WITH SALSA

Preparation Time: 7 minutes   **Cooking Time:** 33 minutes   **Servings:** 4

INGREDIENTS

- 1 cup long-grain white rice
- ¼ cup dried lentils
- 1 cup frozen corn
- 1 cup vegan salsa
- 1 ½ cup canned pinto beans, rinsed and drained
- 1 ¼ cup water
- ½ onion, chopped
- 1 garlic clove, minced
- 1 ½ tablespoon extra-virgin olive oil
- 1 teaspoon chili powder
- ½ teaspoon salt
- ½ teaspoon ground cumin
- Pepper to taste

For the Vegan Salsa:

- ½ cup canned diced tomatoes with green chilies
- ½ cup canned whole tomatoes
- 1/16 cup chopped onion
- 1/8 cup cilantro, chopped
- ½ garlic clove, chopped
- ¼ jalapeno, chopped
- Pinch salt
- 1/8 teaspoon cane sugar

DIRECTIONS

To Prepare the Vegan Salsa:

1. Pour all the ingredients into the food processor. Pulse until the ingredients are well combined. Check for flavor, and add more spices if you want. Pulse until the mixture gets the consistency you like. Set aside.

To Prepare the Rest:

2. Heat the oil in a medium-deep skillet over medium heat. Add the onions and sauté for 3 minutes, until softened. Add the garlic and rice and cook for 2 minutes, stirring occasionally.
3. Pour in the water and salsa; add the pinto beans, lentils, corn, and all the spices. Bring to a boil, stirring occasionally. Reduce the heat, cover the pot and let it simmer for about 20 minutes, until the liquid has been absorbed and the rice tender.
4. Serve immediately.

Nutrition: Calories: 871; Protein 29 g; Carbohydrates 138 g; Fat 26 g; Sugar 0.1 g; Sodium 140 mg

14. SAFFRON GREEN BEANS AND RICE

Preparation Time: 3 minutes   **Cooking Time:** 22 minutes   **Servings:** 4-5

INGREDIENTS

For the Beans and Rice:
- 2 cups rice
- 20 green beans, cut into 1-inch pieces
- 1 cup peas
- 1 cup cauliflower, cut into florets
- 2 carrots, cut into round slices
- 1 onion, sliced
- 2 large potatoes, cut into small cubes
- ½ cup vegetable oil
- 1 ½ cups vegan soy yogurt
- ¼ cup + 2 tablespoons coconut milk, warmed
- 1 teaspoon kewra water
- 1 tablespoon whole spices
- 1 tablespoon chopped mint leaves
- 1 teaspoon saffron, divided
- 1 tablespoon lemon juice
- ½ teaspoon turmeric
- ½ teaspoon black cumin seeds
- 2 teaspoons chili powder
- 2 tablespoons salt
- 2 tablespoons ginger garlic paste
- 2 tablespoons chopped coriander leaves

For the Vegan Soy Yogurt:
- 1 ½ cup soy milk
- ½ cup yogurt starter
- 1 teaspoon agar agar powder

DIRECTIONS

To Prepare the Vegan Soy Yogurt:
1. Preheat the oven to 120°F.
2. In a saucepan, combine the soy milk and agar agar powder. Heat to 195°F but do not boil. It's not necessary, but you can use a thermometer.
3. Pour the mixture into a bowl and leave it to cool to 105°F or 120°F. If not using a thermometer, put your finger in the mixture. It's ready when it's hot but does not burn.
4. Stir in the starter and transfer the mixture into a glass jar or container.
5. Turn off the oven, place the jar (without the lid on) in the oven, and let it stand for at least 8 hours. Do not open the oven during this process.
6. When done, you can keep the soy yogurt in the fridge.

To Prepare the Beans and Rice:
7. Prepare the rice by boiling it in a saucepan filled with water and turmeric, some salt, whole spices, and lemon juice.
8. In a small bowl, combine 2 tablespoons of coconut milk and ½ teaspoon of saffron.
9. When the rice is done, spread on a tray and sprinkle it with the saffron and milk mixture.
10. In a bowl, combine the soy yogurt, kewra water, the remaining saffron, mint leaves, and coriander leaves. Set aside.
11. Heat the oil in a saucepan over medium-high heat. Add the onion and black cumin, then fry until the onion is dark golden. Stir in the chili powder, ginger garlic paste, and salt together with the chopped vegetables.
12. Gradually pour in little water while frying the vegetables. Reduce the heat to low and let it cook until tender. Pour in ½ of the yogurt mixture, stir well and remove from the stove.
13. To assemble the dish, spread half the vegetables in a pan, cover with half rice, and drizzle with 4 tablespoons of the yogurt mixture. Repeat in the same order with the rest of the vegetables, rice, and yogurt mixture.
14. Cover the pot and put over low flame for about 15 minutes.
15. Serve warm.

Nutrition: Calories: 1257; Protein 36 g; Carbohydrates 169 g; Fat 28 g; Sodium 203 mg

15. AFRICAN RICE AND BEANS WITH YAM

Preparation Time: 7 minutes   **Cooking Time:** 22 minutes   **Servings:** 8

INGREDIENTS

- 1 cup black-eyed peas, pre-soaked
- 2 ½ cups rice
- 2 ½ large onions, chopped
- 2 carrots, chopped
- 5 garlic cloves, chopped
- 1 yam, chopped
- 1 vegetable bouillon cube
- ¾ cup tomato paste
- ¼ cup coconut oil
- 2 ½ teaspoons salt
- ¼ teaspoon hot pepper
- Pepper to taste

DIRECTIONS

1. Heat the oil in a big pot over medium-high heat. Add the chopped onions and garlic and sauté until translucent. Pour in the tomato paste and stir well to combine the ingredients.
2. Pour in about 5 cups of water and bring to a boil. Add the beans, yams, carrots, vegetable bouillon cube, hot pepper, salt, and pepper. Cook until the beans become tender.
3. Stir in the rice, cover the pot and cook for 10 minutes. Uncover the pot and cook for another 10 minutes. Do not stir. If it appears to be too dry, pour in some more water. If it is too watery, cover the pot and cook covered for some time.
4. Serve warm.

Nutrition: Calories: 2319; Protein 29 g; Carbohydrates 210 g; Fat 167 g; Sodium 158 mg

16. ARABIC RICE AND BEANS

Preparation Time: 7 minutes   **Cooking Time:** 36 minutes   **Servings:** 4-6

INGREDIENTS

- 1/3 cup basmati rice
- 1 cup lentils
- ¼ cup olive or vegetable oil
- 4 cups water
- 2 large onions, sliced
- 1 teaspoon cumin
- ½ teaspoon black pepper
- Salt to taste

DIRECTIONS

1. Heat the oil in a skillet over medium heat; add the onions and sauté, stirring occasionally, until the onions are golden brown.
2. In another saucepan, add the water, lentils pepper, and salt and cook for about 20 minutes, or until the lentils are tender. Stir in the uncooked rice, cumin, and onions (prepared in step 1), mix well, cover the pan and simmer for 15 minutes more. The dish is done when the rice is tender and the liquid is absorbed.
3. Serve warm.

Nutrition: Calories: 457; Protein: 21 g; Carbohydrates: 132 g; Fat: 19 g; Sodium: 500 mg

17. RICE AND LENTIL DINNER

Preparation Time: 7 minutes   **Cooking Time:** 37 minutes   **Servings:** 4

INGREDIENTS

- 1 can red lentils, drained
- 2 cups brown rice, cooked
- 2 tablespoons extra virgin oil
- 1 tablespoon Dijon mustard
- Pinch smoked paprika
- 1 fresh parsley sprig, chopped
- Salt and pepper

DIRECTIONS

1. Whisk oil, mustard, paprika, salt, and pepper in a bowl.
2. Add beans and rice. Stir to mix.
3. Garnish with parsley before serving.

Nutrition: Calories: 779; Protein 24 g; Carbohydrates 104 g; Fat 31 g; Sodium 456 mg

18. BEAN AND BARLEY STEW

Preparation Time: 7 minutes   **Cooking Time:** 55 minutes   **Servings:** 4

INGREDIENTS

- 1 can white beans, drained
- 1 can diced tomatoes
- 6 cups vegetable broth
- ½ cup quick-cooking barley
- 4 teaspoons extra-virgin olive oil
- 1 medium fennel bulb, chopped
- 1 large onion, chopped
- 5 garlic cloves, crushed
- 4 cups baby spinach
- 1 teaspoon dried basil
- 2 cups parmesan cheese, grated

DIRECTIONS

1. Sauté fennel, onion, garlic, and basil in oil.
2. Add beans, tomatoes, vegetable broth, and barley, then bring to a boil. Stir occasionally.
3. Add spinach and cook until wilted.
4. Top with parmesan cheese before serving.

Nutrition: Calories: 1897; Protein 114 g; Carbohydrates 228 g; Fat 107 g; Sodium 515 mg

19. COWBOY DINNER

Preparation Time: 7 minutes   **Cooking Time:** 33 minutes   **Servings:** 4

INGREDIENTS

- 2 cans kidney beans, water set aside
- 1 pound lean ground beef
- 1 large onion, diced
- 3 garlic cloves, minced
- 2 cups mushrooms, diced
- 3 tablespoons canola oil
- 5 tablespoons taco seasoning

DIRECTIONS

1. Sauté onions and garlic. Add beef and cook until brown.
2. Add beans, mushrooms, and taco seasoning. Add water that you set aside from the beans and let it simmer for 10 minutes.

Nutrition: Calories: 987; Protein 27 g; Carbohydrates 89 g; Fat 19 g; Sodium 572 mg

20. CURRIED BEAN AND RICE

Preparation Time: 7 minutes   **Cooking Time:** 29 minutes   **Servings:** 4

INGREDIENTS

- 1 can brown lentils, drained
- 3 cups basmati rice, cooked
- 4 garlic cloves, crushed
- 2 tablespoon olive oil
- 1 teaspoon fresh ginger paste
- 2 teaspoons red curry paste

DIRECTIONS

1. Sauté ginger and garlic in oil. Add curry paste and cook until fragrant.
2. Add brown lentils and rice; mix well.

Nutrition: Calories: 899; Protein 43 g; Carbohydrates 165 g; Fat 36 g; Sodium 277 mg

21. TUSCAN CANNELLINI BEANS AND RICE

Preparation Time: 7 minutes   **Cooking Time:** 33 minutes   **Servings:** 4-6

INGREDIENTS

- 4 cups low-sodium vegetable broth
- 1 cup brown rice
- 1 ½ cup canned cannellini beans, drained and rinsed
- 2 carrots, diced
- ½ large onion, diced
- 1 garlic clove, minced
- 2 stalks celery, diced
- 2 cups baby spinach leaves
- 2/3 cup canned tomato paste
- 1 tablespoon extra-virgin olive oil
- ½ teaspoon herbs de Provence
- 2 teaspoons chopped fresh sage leaves
- 1 tablespoon chopped fresh thyme leaves
- ¼ teaspoon freshly ground black pepper
- ½ teaspoon sea salt

DIRECTIONS

1. Cook the rice until crispy and tender. It should not be completely done.
2. In a large pot, heat the olive oil over medium heat. Add the carrots, onions, garlic, spinach, thyme, herbs de Provence, sage, pepper, and salt. Cook for about 5 minutes, stirring occasionally until the vegetables are tender.
3. Pour in the tomato paste and the vegetable broth and bring to a boil. Stir in the rice and beans, reduce the heat to low, and simmer for 10-15 minutes.
4. Serve warm.

Nutrition: Calories: 865; Carbohydrates 126 g; Protein 25 g; Fat 26 g; Sugar 7 g; Sodium 150 mg

22. FRUITY BEANS AND RICE

Preparation Time: 6 minutes   **Cooking Time:** 20 minutes   **Servings:** 4-6

INGREDIENTS

- ½ cup rice
- 3 cups canned kidney beans, drained
- 1 plump vine tomato, coarsely chopped
- 1 ½ cup boiling water
- 12 prunes, pitted
- 6 dried apricots
- 1/3 cup sultanas or raisins
- 1 medium onion, finely chopped
- 1-2 green chilies, finely chopped
- 4 garlic cloves, finely chopped
- 1 (1-inch) ginger piece, peeled, finely chopped
- 1 small green pepper, coarsely chopped
- 1 cinnamon stick (approximately 3-inch piece)
- 1 ripe banana, thinly sliced
- ¼ cup chopped toasted peanuts
- 2 tablespoons sunflower oil
- 1 teaspoon ground coriander
- 1 teaspoon ground cumin
- 1 teaspoon fennel seed
- Lemon wedges, for topping

DIRECTIONS

1. Bring a saucepan filled with water to a boil. Add the rice, reduce the heat and simmer until the rice is tender. When done, cover the pan and keep it warm.
2. In a small saucepan, add the boiling water along with the dried fruit. Cover the pan and bring it to a boil. Reduce the heat and simmer for about 20 minutes or until plump. Do not drain the fruit.
3. In the meantime, heat a large saucepan and pour in the oil. Add the onions and fry until lightly golden. Stir in the chilies, garlic, green pepper, ginger, and all the spices. Cook for about 1-2 minutes, stirring frequently.
4. Add the kidney beans, chopped tomatoes, and salt. Stir in the fruit together with the water. When it starts boiling, reduce the heat and simmer for 30 minutes, stirring occasionally.
5. Serve warm, on top of the cooked rice. Sprinkle with the toasted peanuts, lemon wedges, and a few slices of banana.

Nutrition: Calories: 116; Carbohydrates 165 g; Protein 47 g; Fat 43 g,; Sugar 5 g; Sodium 320 mg

23. RICE AND BEANS COLORFUL DISH

Preparation Time: 7 minutes   **Cooking Time:** 43 minutes   **Servings:** 6-8

INGREDIENTS

- ½ cup rice
- ½ cup raisins
- 1 medium red onion, diced
- 1 large carrot, grated
- 1 medium red bell pepper, diced
- 1 ½ cups canned black beans, rinsed and drained
- 1 cup snow peas
- 1 teaspoon raw sugar
- 2 tablespoons lime juice
- ½ teaspoon salt
- 2 tablespoons olive oil
- 1 teaspoon dried ginger
- 2 tablespoons chopped cilantro

DIRECTIONS

1. In a small bowl, whisk lime juice, salt, and sugar until dissolved. Set aside.
2. Prepare the rice according to the package directions.
3. Meanwhile, in a wide skillet, heat the oil; add the onion, carrot, and red pepper. Sauté for 5 minutes, until tender. Stir in the ginger and peas and cook until the peas turn bright green, stirring frequently. And the black beans, stir well and remove from the heat.
4. When the rice is done, stir in the raisins and transfer the mixture into the skillet. Stir well to combine the rice and vegetables. Drizzle with lime juice and stir well again.
5. Serve immediately with some chopped cilantro.

Nutrition: Calories: 657; Carbohydrates 104 g; Protein 35 g; Fat 25 g; Sugar 1 g; Sodium 397 mg

24. RICE AND CHILI BEAN POT

Preparation Time: 7 minutes   **Cooking Time:** 43 minutes   **Servings:** 6

INGREDIENTS

- 1 ¾ cup canned kidney beans, drained and rinsed
- 3 cups canned diced tomatoes
- 1 cup wild rice
- 1 large brown onion, finely chopped
- 1 green capsicum, chopped
- 2 garlic cloves, crushed
- 2 celery sticks, sliced
- ¾ cups thickly sliced mushrooms
- ½ cup water
- 4 tablespoons chili con carne mix
- 2 teaspoons olive oil
- 2 tablespoons tomato paste

DIRECTIONS

1. Prepare the rice according to the package directions.
2. In a large saucepan heat the oil over medium heat.
3. Add the garlic and onion and cook for about 5 minutes, until tender. Stir in the capsicum, tomato paste, chili con carne mix, and mushrooms, then pour in the water. Cook, stirring occasionally for 5 minutes.
4. Add the tomatoes and kidney beans and bring to a boil. Reduce the heat to medium-low and simmer for about 35 minutes, or until the mixture thickens. Season with salt and pepper and serve warm.
5. To serve, spoon the wild rice into the bowls and top with the bean mixture.

Nutrition: Calories: 927; Protein 48 g; Carbohydrates 163 g; Fat 21 g; Sodium 180 mg

25. RED LENTILS

Preparation Time: 8 minutes   **Cooking Time:** 8 minutes   **Servings:** 8

INGREDIENTS

- 2 cups red lentils, rinsed
- 4 cups chicken broth
- 2 small brown onions, chopped finely

DIRECTIONS

1. In a Dutch oven, add lentils, onion, and broth over high heat and cook until boiling. Now, set the heat to low and cook for about 5 minutes.
2. In 4 (1 pint) hot sterilized jars, divide the lentils. Fill each jar with hot cooking liquid, leaving a 1-inch space from the top.
3. Run your knife around the insides of each jar to remove any air bubbles. Clean any trace of food off the rims of jars with a clean, moist kitchen towel.
4. Close each jar with a lid and screw on the ring. Carefully place the jars in the pressure canner and process at 10 pounds pressure for about 75 minutes.
5. Remove the jars from the pressure canner and place them onto a wooden surface several inches apart to cool completely.
6. After cooling with your finger, press the top of each jar's lid to ensure that the seal is tight. Store these canning jars in a cool, dark place.

Nutrition: Calories: 776; Carbohydrates 106 g; Protein 59 g; Fat 2 g

26. DIRTY SPICE RICE

Preparation Time: 10 minutes   **Cooking Time:** 30 minutes   **Servings:** 4

INGREDIENTS

- 2 tablespoons olive oil
- 3 garlic cloves, minced
- 1 chopped onion
- 1 green bell pepper, chopped
- 1 tablespoon chili powder
- 2 teaspoons annatto powder
- ¼ teaspoon crushed red pepper flakes
- 1 teaspoon ground cumin
- ¼ teaspoon ground cinnamon
- 1-½ cups uncooked white rice
- 3 cups water
- 3 large tomatoes, chopped
- 1 can black beans, rinsed and drained
- ¼ cup toasted pine nuts
- 1 red onion, sliced
- 1 tablespoon lime juice

DIRECTIONS

1. Place a large pan over medium heat and add 1 table-spoon of olive oil.
2. Add the garlic and onion. Cook for 4-5 minutes, stirring frequently.
3. Add the pepper, chili powder, chili flakes, annatto, cinnamon, and cumin. Cook for 2-3 minutes stirring continually.
4. Mix in the rice and ensure it is well coated. Once everything is well mixed add the water and a sprinkling of sea salt.
5. Bring the boil then reduce the heat, cover and let simmer for 23-25 minutes.
6. Once the rice is cooked and the water is all gone add the tomatoes, red onion, cilantro, black beans, pine nuts, and the remaining olive oil. Mix everything and cook for 3-5 minutes, or until everything is heated through.
7. Drizzle the lime juice over the top.

Nutrition: Calories: 797; Carbohydrates 112 g; Protein 27 g; Fat 29 g; Fiber: 0.9 g; Sugar 1.5 g; Sodium 97 mg

27. TASTY BEANS AND RICE

Preparation Time: 7 minutes   **Cooking Time:** 43 minutes   **Servings:** 2-4

INGREDIENTS

- 1 cup dry brown rice
- 1 ½ cup canned great northern white beans, drained and rinsed
- 1 garlic clove, minced
- 1 onion, chopped
- 1 tablespoon vegetable oil
- ¼ cup canned black olives
- 2 celery stalks, chopped
- 1/3 cup fresh chopped parsley
- 1 lemon, juiced
- 2 teaspoons dry dill weed

DIRECTIONS

1. Cook the rice following the package directions.
2. Heat the oil in a large pan over medium-high heat. Add the onion and sauté for 5 minutes. Place the garlic and cook for 5 minutes more. Add the beans and cook until heated through. Stir in the olives and celery, then fry for a few minutes more, until the celery and olives are softened. Add the parsley and lemon juice. Mix well.
3. When the rice is done, stir in the dill. Season with salt and pepper. Add the cooked rice to the bean mixture and mix well.
4. Serve immediately with some pita bread.

Nutrition: Calories: 519; Protein 50 g; Carbohydrates 168 g; Fat 5 g; Sugar 0.1 g; Sodium 121 mg

28. THAI-STYLE BEANS AND RICE WITH COCONUT MILK

Preparation Time: 7 minutes   **Cooking Time:** 33 minutes   **Servings:** 4-6

INGREDIENTS

- 1 ½ cup canned red kidney beans, drained and rinsed
- 1 ¾ cup canned diced tomatoes, undrained
- 1 ½ cup unsweetened coconut milk
- 2 ½ cups basmati rice
- 1 small red bell pepper, seeded and chopped
- 1 medium onion, chopped
- 2 tablespoons fresh minced garlic
- 1-2 tablespoons red curry paste
- 3 tablespoons vegetable oil
- 1-2 tablespoons sugar
- 2 tablespoons fresh lime juice
- Salt and black pepper to taste
- 1 chopped green onion, for garnish

DIRECTIONS

1. Bring to a boil a pot filled with water. Add the rice, reduce the heat and simmer until the rice is tender.
2. In the meantime, heat the oil in a Dutch oven over medium-high heat. Add the bell pepper and onions. Sauté for about 5 minutes. 2 minutes before the onions are done, stir in the garlic. Add the red curry paste and cook for 1 more minute.
3. Pour in the coconut milk and lime juice; add the kidney beans, sugar, and diced tomatoes. When it starts boiling, reduce the heat and let it simmer for 35 minutes.
4. When done, season with salt and pepper.
5. Serve immediately over hot rice and sprinkle with chopped green onion.

Nutrition: Calories: 873; Carbohydrates 148 g; Protein 30 g; Fat 54 g; Sugar 2.1 g; Sodium 200 mg

29. TOFU AND RICE AND LENTILS CURRY

Preparation Time: 7 minutes   **Cooking Time:** 43 minutes   **Servings:** 4

INGREDIENTS

- ½ cup spit red lentils
- 1 cup chopped green beans, topped
- 10 ounces firm tofu, chopped
- 1/3 cup chopped fresh coriander
- 1 cup basmati rice
- 1 medium brown onion, chopped
- 2 ½ cups vegetable stock
- 11 ounces cauliflower, cut into florets
- 2 medium carrots, peeled and sliced
- 1 (10-inch) ginger piece, peeled and finely chopped
- 1 large fresh chili, halved, deseeded, chopped
- 2 teaspoons garam masala
- 1 teaspoon ground turmeric
- Salt and pepper to taste

DIRECTIONS

1. Bring to a boil a saucepan filled with water. Reduce the heat, add the rice and cook until tender.
2. In a large saucepan, heat the oil over medium heat. Add the onion and sauté for 5 minutes. When the onion is soft, add the ginger, garam masala, and turmeric and cook for 1 minute, stirring.
3. Pour in the vegetable stock; add the cauliflower, lentils, chili, and carrots. Bring to a boil, reduce the heat to medium-low, and simmer, covered for about 15 minutes. Add the beans and tofu and cook for 10 minutes more.
4. When the vegetables are done, season with salt and pepper and gently stir the coriander.
5. Serve immediately with hot rice.

Nutrition: Calories: 1421; Carbohydrates 267 g; Protein 56 g; Fat 18 g; Sugar 0 g; Sodium 433 mg

30. SPICY RICE AND BEANS

Preparation Time: 6 minutes   **Cooking Time:** 22 minutes   **Servings:** 6-8

INGREDIENTS

- 1 ½ cup canned pinto beans, drained
- 1 ½ cup long-grain brown rice
- 2 ¾ cups water
- ½ cup grated carrot
- ½ cup chopped celery
- 1 cup chopped onion
- ½ cup fresh corn (or ½ cup frozen corn)
- 1 cup chopped tomato
- 3 garlic cloves, smashed
- 1 jalapeno pepper, seeded, finely diced
- 1 teaspoon ground cumin
- 1 tablespoon canola oil
- 2 teaspoons chili powder
- 1 teaspoon ground coriander
- 1 bay leaf
- 1 tablespoon vegetable bouillon granules
- 2 tablespoons fresh parsley
- 1 tablespoon chopped fresh cilantro (optional)

DIRECTIONS

1. Pour the canola oil into a large frying pan and heat it over medium heat. Add the garlic, onion, jalapeno pepper, and celery. Sauté for 3 minutes, stirring occasionally. Stir in the chili powder, coriander, cumin, and rice. Cook on medium heat, until golden, stirring occasionally.
2. Add the carrot, bay leaf, and bouillon powder and pour in water. Cover the pan and simmer for about 20 minutes.
3. Stir in the tomato, beans, and corn. Cover the pot again and simmer for 15-20 minutes more, until the liquid has been absorbed.
4. When done, remove and discard the bay leaf. Add the chopped cilantro (optional) and 1 tablespoon of parsley.
5. Serve warm and garnish with the remaining parsley.

Nutrition: Calories: 876; Carbohydrates 156 g; Protein 38 g; Fat 25 g; Sugar 5 g; Sodium 5 mg

31. LENTIL AND RICE BURRITO

Preparation Time: 7 minutes   **Cooking Time:** 33 minutes   **Servings:** 4

INGREDIENTS

- 2 cups cooked lentils
- 2 tablespoons taco seasoning mix
- 1/4 cup water
- 8 large soft tortillas
- 2-3 cups shredded cheese (preferred)
- 1 salsa jar (preferred)
- 2 cups rice

DIRECTIONS

1. In a large skillet, heat lentils on low-to-medium heat. Add taco seasoning and water and incorporate them into lentils. Simmer for about 5 minutes until the mixture heats through and thickens.
2. Top each tortilla evenly with the lentil mixture and top with rice, salsa, and cheese. Fold into a burrito. Heat in the oven if desired (350°F for approximately 10 minutes). Serve with more salsa if desired.

Nutrition: Calories: 969; Carbohydrates 183 g; Protein 27 g; Fat 56 g; Sodium 186 mg

CHAPTER 3
SURVIVAL BEANS RECIPES

32. CANNED CHICKPEAS

Preparation Time: 5 minutes   **Cooking Time:** 35 minutes   **Servings:** 5

INGREDIENTS

- 2 ¼ pounds chickpeas
- ½ tablespoon salt (for each jar)
- Water, as required

DIRECTIONS

1. Wash the chickpeas and cover them with water in a pan. Bring them to a boil for 2 minutes. Remove the chickpeas from the heat and soak them for 1 hour.
2. Drain the chickpeas and add more water to cover them. Boil the chickpeas for 30 minutes more.
3. Pack the chickpeas in jars, leaving 1-inch headspace. Add ½ tablespoon of salt in each jar, then add the cooking liquid to cover the beans.
4. Remove the air bubbles and wipe the jar rims. Place the lids and rings on.
5. Process the pint jars for 60 minutes in the pressure canner at 10 pounds pressure.
6. Wait for the pressure canner to depressurize before removing the jars.

Nutrition: Calories: 735; Carbohydrates 167 g; Protein 33 g; Fat 16 g; Fiber: 24.6 g

33. BAKED FETA BEAN TOMATOES

Preparation Time: 15 minutes   **Cooking Time:** 25 minutes   **Servings:** 2

INGREDIENTS

- 2 tablespoons tomato paste
- 1 (14 ounces) can butter beans, drained, and rinsed; or 5 ounces dry butter beans, soaked and cooked
- 1 (14 ounces) can chickpeas, drained and rinsed; or 5 ounces dry chickpeas, soaked and cooked
- 6 garlic cloves, peeled
- 14 ounces heirloom tomatoes, chopped so they're all roughly the same size
- 4 ½ ounces cherry truss tomatoes
- 2 teaspoons smoked paprika
- ¼ cup extra-virgin olive oil, divided
- 2 tablespoons pomegranate molasses, divided
- 3 ½ ounces Greek feta cheese, crumbled
- Tabasco and sliced baguettes, to serve
- Cooking spray

DIRECTIONS

1. Preheat oven to 425°F (220°C).
2. Grease a baking dish with cooking spray or cooking oil.
3. To the baking dish, add the tomato paste, butter beans, chickpeas, garlic, tomatoes, paprika, 2 tablespoons of oil, and 1 ½ tablespoon of molasses.
4. Bake until tomatoes soften, about 30 minutes.
5. Stir to break tomatoes gently, then bake for 10 minutes more until tomatoes start to release juices.
6. Remove from the oven and drizzle the remaining oil and molasses over the tomatoes. Top with feta cheese.
7. Serve with tabasco and sliced baguettes.

Nutrition: Calories: 987 g; Carbohydrates 183 g; Protein 34 g; Fat 38 g; Sodium 854 mg

34. WHITE BEAN AVOCADO TOAST

Preparation Time: 15 minutes   **Cooking Time:** 20 minutes   **Servings:** 2

INGREDIENTS

- 1 tablespoon olive oil
- 3 garlic cloves, minced
- 1 (15 ounces) can cannellini beans (white kidney beans), drained and rinsed; or 5 ounces dry cannellini beans, soaked and cooked
- ½ teaspoon kosher salt, or to taste
- Freshly ground black pepper, to taste
- ½ teaspoon dried oregano
- 2 avocados, pitted, peeled, and chopped
- 4 slices hearty whole-grain bread, toasted
- BBQ sauce, to taste
- Hemp seeds, to taste

DIRECTIONS

1. In a medium saucepan or skillet, heat oil over medium heat.
2. Add the garlic and cook until fragrant, about 1-2 minutes.
3. Add the beans, freshly ground black pepper, salt, and oregano. Cook for 4-5 minutes.
4. In a small bowl, mash the chopped avocado.
5. Spread the mashed avocado evenly over the bread slices, then top with the bean mixture.
6. Top with the BBQ sauce and hemp seeds, then serve.

Nutrition: Calories: 527; Carbohydrates 192 g; Protein 35 g; Fat 47 g; Sodium 142 mg

35. CRANBERRY BEANS

Preparation Time: 5 minutes   **Cooking Time:** 60 minutes   **Servings:** 4

INGREDIENTS

- 2 pounds shelled cranberry beans
- 3 chopped garlic cloves
- ¾ cup white wine
- 4 tablespoons lemon juice
- 6 tablespoons olive oil
- 6 teaspoons fresh marjoram
- ½ teaspoon black pepper
- ¾ teaspoon salt
- 2 cups chicken stock

DIRECTIONS

1. Prepare the canning jars following the directions in chapter 3.
2. In a large container, combine the beans with all ingredients except the chicken stock.
3. Pack beans into each canning jar and add chicken broth. Remember to leave a one-inch headspace. Use a spatula to remove air bubbles, then use a clean cloth to wipe jar rims. After that, adjust the lids and screw band.
4. Set your filled jars in the pressure canner at 11 pounds for dial-gauge or 10 pounds for the weighted canner. Process heat jars for 60 minutes, adjusting for altitude. Switch off the heat and let the pressure drop naturally. Remove the lid and allow the jars to cool in the canner for 5 minutes. Take out the jars and cool them further. Inspect lid seals after 24 hours.

Nutrition: Calories: 746; Carbohydrates 185 g; Protein 33 g; Fat 57 g; Sodium 320 mg

36. BACON BEANS

Preparation Time: 15 minutes   **Cooking Time:** 23 minutes   **Servings:** 4

INGREDIENTS

- 3 slices thick-cut bacon
- 2 pints canned green beans

DIRECTIONS

1. Boil green beans in water for 10 minutes, then drain.
2. Fry bacon until crispy in a skillet over medium-high heat.
3. Remove bacon and reserve about half of the grease.
4. Chop bacon finely and return to skillet.
5. Add drained beans to skillet and cook for 5 minutes, stirring and tossing.

Nutrition: Calories: 343; Carbohydrates 186 g; Protein 28 g; Fat 19 g

37. BLACK EYED PEAS

Preparation Time: 5 minutes   **Cooking Time:** 75 minutes   **Servings:** 4

INGREDIENTS

- 1 ½ pound dried black-eyed peas
- 6 tablespoons chopped onions
- 30 peppercorns
- ¾ teaspoon dried herbs (preferred)
- 1 teaspoon salt

DIRECTIONS

1. Rinse and soak peas overnight.
2. Add rinsed beans to a large saucepot and cover with fresh water. Boil for 30 minutes.
3. Pack beans into each canning jar, distribute all ingredients evenly; and, add boiling water. Remember to leave a 1-inch headspace. Use a spatula to remove air bubbles, then use a clean cloth to wipe jar rims. After that, adjust the lids and screw band.
4. Set your filled jars in the pressure canner at 11 pounds for dial-gauge or 10 pounds for the weighted canner. Process heat jars for 75 minutes, adjusting for altitude. Switch off the heat and let the pressure drop naturally. Remove the lid and allow the jars to cool in the canner for 5 minutes. Take out the jars and cool them further. Inspect lid seals after 24 hours.

Nutrition: Calories: 219; Carbohydrates 95 g; Protein 15 g; Fat 11 g; Fiber: 1.9 g; Sodium 272 mg

38. CANNED DILL GREEN BEANS

Preparation Time: 15 minutes   **Cooking Time:** 23 minutes   **Servings:** 4 pints

INGREDIENTS

- 5 cups water
- 5 cups cider vinegar
- 1/2 cup pickling salt
- 1 garlic clove (for each jar)
- 1/2 teaspoon dill seed (for each jar)
- 1/2 teaspoon mustard seed (for each jar)
- 1/4 teaspoon red pepper flakes (for each jar)
- 4 pounds yellow or green beans (for each jar)

DIRECTIONS

1. Boil water with pickling salt and vinegar to form a brine.
2. Add 1/2 teaspoon of dill seed, 1/4 teaspoon of red pepper flakes, 1 garlic clove, and 1/2 teaspoon of mustard seed to each jar.
3. Fill jars, packed tightly, with beans; leave a 1-inch space at the top.
4. Pour boiling brine over the beans to the top of the jar.
5. Close the lids and place them into the pressure canner.
6. Place on rack in the pressure canner and fill to just below the rings of the jars with hot water.
7. Close and heat to boiling, then put the weighted pressure gauge on top of the canner and reduce heat.
8. Process at 11 psi for 5-10 minutes. Let cool to room temperature.

Nutrition: Calories: 567; Carbohydrates 238 g; Protein 65 g; Fat 53 g

39. KALE BEAN POTATO HASH

Preparation Time: 15 minutes   **Cooking Time:** 25 minutes   **Servings:** 2

INGREDIENTS

- 3 medium Yukon Gold potatoes, diced into ½ inch cubes
- 1 tablespoon avocado oil
- ½ red bell pepper, cored and diced
- ½ cup vegan breakfast sausage, chopped (optional)
- 2 garlic cloves, minced
- ½ large onion, finely diced
- ½ (8 ounces) can black beans, drained and rinsed; or 2.5 ounces dry black beans, soaked and cooked
- 2 heaping cups kale, stemmed and chopped
- 1 teaspoon Old Bay seasoning, or to taste
- Freshly ground black pepper and kosher salt, to taste
- Handful cilantro or flat-leaf parsley, finely chopped
- 1 large avocado, pitted and sliced, to serve
- Toasted bread, to serve

DIRECTIONS

1. Cook the potatoes in boiling water for 4-5 minutes; drain and set aside.
2. In a medium saucepan or skillet, heat oil over medium heat.
3. Add the potatoes and cook until browned, about 4-5 minutes.
4. Add the bell pepper, vegan sausage, garlic, onion, and Old Bay seasoning. Mix until well combined.
5. Cook for 8-10 minutes until potatoes are cooked through.
6. Add the beans and kale; cook until kale wilts, about 2 minutes.
7. Season with freshly ground black pepper and salt, then top with the chopped cilantro/parsley.
8. Serve warm with the toasted bread and avocado slices.

Nutrition: Calories: 569; Carbohydrates 187 g; Protein 47 g; Fat 36 g; Sodium 228 mg

40. ARUGULA LIMA BEAN FRITTATA

Preparation Time: 15 minutes   **Cooking Time:** 25 minutes   **Servings:** 2

INGREDIENTS

- ⅓ cup unsweetened almond milk
- 8 large eggs
- ⅛ teaspoon kosher salt
- ½ teaspoon freshly ground black pepper
- ½ teaspoon chili powder
- ½ teaspoon paprika
- 1 teaspoon extra-virgin olive oil
- ¼ cup scallions, chopped
- 1 cup arugula
- ⅓ cup dry lima beans, soaked and cooked
- 1 large carrot, peeled and grated
- ½ cup cherry tomatoes, chopped
- 1 tablespoon dried thyme

DIRECTIONS

1. Preheat oven to 350°F (175°C).
2. In a large mixing bowl, add the almond milk, eggs, salt, chili powder, freshly ground black pepper, and paprika. Mix well.
3. In a medium saucepan or skillet, heat oil over medium heat.
4. Add the scallions, arugula, beans, carrots, and tomatoes. Cook for 6-8 minutes until softened.
5. Pour the egg mixture and cook for a few seconds.
6. Add the thyme, stir, then remove from heat.
7. Place the mixture into a baking pan; bake until eggs are firm, about 12-15 minutes.
8. Slice and serve warm.

Nutrition: Calories: 876; Carbohydrates 159 g; Protein 87 g; Fat 54 g; Sodium 260 mg

41. BLUEBERRY BEAN SMOOTHIE

Preparation Time: 15 minutes   **Cooking Time:** 25 minutes   **Servings:** 2

INGREDIENTS

- 1 (15.5 ounces) can cannellini beans, drained and rinsed; or 5 ounces dry cannellini beans, soaked and cooked
- 1 medium frozen banana, peeled
- 1 cup frozen blueberries
- ½ cup plain Greek yogurt
- 1 ½ cup vanilla-flavored almond milk

DIRECTIONS

1. In a food processor or blender, add all the smoothie ingredients.
2. Blend until you get a smooth, rich mixture.
3. In a tall glass, pour the freshly made smoothie and enjoy.

Nutrition: Calories: 987; Fat 62 g; Carbohydrates 235 g; Protein 38 g; Sodium 352 mg

42. BLACK BEAN CHOCOLATE SMOOTHIE

Preparation Time: 15 minutes   **Cooking Time:** 25 minutes   **Servings:** 2

INGREDIENTS

- 2 bananas, frozen and chopped
- ½ cup cooked black beans (pre-soaked), drained
- 4 Medjool dates, pitted
- 1 tablespoon cashew butter
- 2 tablespoons cocoa/cacao powder
- 1 ½ cup soy milk (or preferred)

DIRECTIONS

1. In a food processor or blender, add all the smoothie ingredients.
2. Blend until you get a smooth, rich mixture.
3. In a tall glass, pour the freshly made smoothie and enjoy.

Nutrition: Calories: 562; Carbohydrates 149 g; Protein 26 g; Fat 25 g; Sodium 115 mg

43. BLACK BEAN SALAD

Preparation Time: 15 minutes   **Cooking Time:** 25 minutes   **Servings:** 2

INGREDIENTS

- 1 can black beans, drained and rinsed
- 1 ½ cup frozen corn, defrosted
- ½ cup chopped green onion
- 2 jalapeno peppers, seeded and chopped finely
- 3 large tomatoes, chopped
- 1 avocado, peeled, stone removed, and cut into chunks
- ¼ cup chopped basil
- 1 lime, juiced
- 1 tablespoon olive oil
- 1 teaspoon sugar
- Sea salt and ground black pepper, to taste

DIRECTIONS

1. In a large bowl mix all the ingredients except the sugar, pepper, and salt.
2. Make sure the salad is well-tossed and mixed before sprinkling in the remaining ingredients.

Nutrition: Calories: 827; Carbohydrates 176 g; Protein 21 g; Fat 32 g

44. CANNELLINI BEAN TUNA SALAD

Preparation Time: 15 minutes   **Cooking Time:** 25 minutes   **Servings:** 4

INGREDIENTS

- 1 red onion, sliced
- 1 lemon, juiced and zested
- 1 lime, juiced and zested
- 2 cans tuna, drained
- 2 cans cannellini beans, drained and rinsed
- ½ cup chopped mint
- 4 splashes tabasco sauce
- 3 tablespoons olive oil
- Sea salt and ground black pepper, to taste

DIRECTIONS

1. Add all the ingredients to a large mixing bowl, except the olive oil, salt, and pepper. Toss everything well.
2. Once the ingredients are well mixed, season with the remaining ingredients and toss once or twice.

Nutrition: Calories: 453; Carbohydrates 163 g; Protein 43 g; Fat 32 g

45. TUSCAN ARTICHOKE BEAN SKILLET

Preparation Time: 15 minutes   **Cooking Time:** 25 minutes   **Servings:** 2

INGREDIENTS

- 2 tablespoons extra-virgin olive oil, divided
- 8 ounces brown mushrooms, sliced
- 1 ½ cup yellow onion (about 1 large onion), diced
- 3 garlic cloves, minced
- ⅔ cup oil-packed sun-dried tomatoes, drained and chopped
- 1 (14.5 ounces) can artichoke hearts, rinsed and quartered
- 2 (14.5 ounces) cans fire-roasted diced tomatoes with their juices
- 2 (14.5 ounces) cans cannellini beans, drained and rinsed; or 10 ounces dry cannellini beans, soaked and cooked
- ½ teaspoon kosher salt
- ½ teaspoon freshly ground black pepper
- 1 teaspoon dried oregano
- ½ teaspoon dried thyme
- 1 teaspoon granulated sugar
- Chopped flat-leaf parsley, for garnish
- Crusty bread, to serve

DIRECTIONS

1. In a medium saucepan or skillet, heat 1 tablespoon oil over medium heat.
2. Add the mushrooms and cook until softened and evenly browned, about 3-4 minutes. Set aside.
3. Add the remaining oil and onion. Cook until softened and lightly browned, about 2-3 minutes.
4. Add the garlic and sun-dried tomatoes. Cook until fragrant and softened about 2 minutes.
5. Add the artichoke hearts, diced tomatoes with their juices, beans, thyme, oregano, freshly ground black pepper, kosher salt, and sugar.
6. Over medium-low heat, cover, and simmer for about 10 minutes or until warmed through.
7. Add the mushrooms back to the pan and stir gently.
8. Top with parsley and serve warm with some crusty bread.

Nutrition: Calories: 664; Carbohydrates 258 g; Protein 46 g; Fat 32 g; Sodium 539 mg

46. WHITE BEAN CHERRY TOMATO SALAD

Preparation Time: 10 minutes   **Cooking Time:** 5 minutes   **Servings:** 2

INGREDIENTS

- 1 can white beans, drained and rinsed
- 2 cups cherry tomatoes, halved
- ¼ cup chopped parsley
- 1 tablespoon olive oil
- Sea salt and ground black pepper, to taste

DIRECTIONS

1. Add all the ingredients to a large mixing bowl and toss well.

Nutrition: Calories: 259; Carbohydrates 127 g; Protein 21 g; Fat 11 g

47. BEETROOT AND FETA SALAD

Preparation Time: 10 minutes   **Cooking Time:** 0 minutes   **Servings:** 2

INGREDIENTS

- 2 tablespoons olive oil
- ½ cup beetroot
- ½ onion, chopped
- 1 red onion, chopped
- 1 cup puy lentils, cooked
- 2 cups spinach, torn
- ½ cup feta cheese, crumbled or torn
- Ground black pepper, to taste

DIRECTIONS

2. Add the beetroot, onion, lentils, and spinach to a large mixing bowl. Toss well.
3. Add the feta cheese and gently toss to mix.
4. Season with olive oil and black pepper.

Nutrition: Calories: 421; Carbohydrates 169 g; Protein 32 g; Fat 16 g

48. CRANBERRY AND LENTIL SALAD

Preparation Time: 10 minutes   **Cooking Time:** 0 minutes   **Servings:** 2

INGREDIENTS

- 2 cups green or puy lentils, cooked
- ½ cup dried cranberries
- ½ cup walnuts, chopped or crushed
- ½ cup feta cheese, crumbled or torn
- 1 tablespoon chopped parsley
- 3 tablespoons olive oil
- 2 teaspoons lemon juice
- 2 teaspoons honey
- Sea salt and ground black pepper, to taste

DIRECTIONS

1. Add the lentils, cranberries, walnuts, lemon juice, and olive oil to a large mixing bowl. Toss to mix well.
2. In a separate bowl gently mix the honey and feta cheese.
3. Pour the cheese and honey over the salad and gently toss.
4. Season with salt and pepper.

Nutrition: Calories: 748; Carbohydrates 148 g; Protein 27 g; Fat 27 g

49. GREEN BEAN CASSEROLE

Preparation Time: 15 minutes   **Cooking Time:** 35 minutes   **Servings:** 6

INGREDIENTS

- 1 can condensed cream of mushroom soup
- 1/4 teaspoon black pepper
- 1 pint canned green beans
- 3/4 cup milk
- 1 1/3 cup French fried onions

DIRECTIONS

1. Preheat oven to 350°F.
2. In a large baking dish, stir together soup, pepper, and milk.
3. Add beans and 2/3 cup onions and stir again.
4. Bake for 30 minutes.

Nutrition: Calories: 219; Carbohydrates 89 g; Protein 19 g; Fat 15 g

50. GREEN GARLIC BEANS

Preparation Time: 15 minutes   **Cooking Time:** 23 minutes   **Servings:** 5 pints

INGREDIENTS

- 3 tablespoons olive oil
- 1 tablespoon butter
- 1 garlic head, sliced and peeled
- 1/4 cup grated Parmesan
- 30 ounces canned green beans, drained

DIRECTIONS

1. Melt butter with olive oil in a skillet over medium heat.
2. Cook garlic for 1 minute in the skillet.
3. Add green beans and cook for 10 minutes.

Nutrition: Calories: 256; Carbohydrates 198 g; Protein 56 g; Fat 53 g

51. MARINATED FAVA BEANS

Preparation Time: 15 minutes   **Cooking Time:** 25 minutes   **Servings:** 2

INGREDIENTS

- 1 ½ pound fava beans
- 2 tablespoons red wine vinegar
- 1/4 teaspoon black pepper, ground
- 1/2 teaspoon kosher salt
- 2 fresh rosemary sprigs
- 1 teaspoon fresh and minced garlic
- 2 tablespoons olive oil

DIRECTIONS

1. Boil salted water. While water is heating up, remove beans from their pods. Once the water is boiling add beans, and cook for about 3 minutes or until tender and green.
2. Drain the beans and rinse them under cold water. Pop the fava beans out of their casings and set them aside.
3. Mix the vinegar, garlic, olive oil, rosemary sprigs, salt, and pepper in a mason jar. Place the lid on the jar and shake the contents to combine. Add fava beans to the jar and secure the lid. These marinated beans will keep up to three days in the fridge. Allow the beans to soak for at least 15 minutes in the mix before serving them.

Nutrition: Calories: 1009; Carbohydrates 285 g; Protein 59 g; Fat 16 g

52. PASTA E FAGIOLI

Preparation Time: 7 minutes   **Cooking Time:** 33 minutes   **Servings:** 4

INGREDIENTS

- 2 cans cannelloni beans, drained
- 1 can peeled plum tomatoes, crushed
- 1 pound cooked ditalini pasta, cooking water reserved
- 5 tablespoons olive oil
- 2 garlic cloves, minced
- 1/8 teaspoon chili flakes
- Salt and pepper, to taste

DIRECTIONS

1. Sauté garlic and chili flakes in oil until garlic gets color.
2. Add crushed tomatoes and simmer for 5 minutes.
3. Stir in beans and pasta cooking water and bring to a boil Add cooked pasta.
4. Season with salt and pepper before serving.

Nutrition: Calories: 1345; Carbohydrates 199 g; Protein 111 g; Fat 36 g; Sodium 330 mg

53. COCONUT BEAN RICE

Preparation Time: 10 minutes   **Cooking Time:** 30 minutes   **Servings:** 4

INGREDIENTS

- 2 tablespoons vegetable oil
- ½ medium yellow onion, chopped
- 4 garlic cloves, chopped
- 2 cups long-grain rice
- 2 cups full-fat unsweetened coconut milk
- 1 cup water
- 1 cup low-sodium chicken stock or vegetable stock
- 1 teaspoon kosher salt
- 1 teaspoon fresh ginger, grated
- 1 (15 ounces) can kidney beans, drained and rinsed; or 5 ounces dry kidney beans, soaked and cooked
- 2 teaspoons dried thyme
- 1 Scotch bonnet or whole habanero chili
- Lime wedges, to serve (optional)

DIRECTIONS

1. In a medium saucepan or skillet, heat oil over medium heat.
2. Add the onion and cook until softened and translucent, about 4-5 minutes.
3. Place the garlic and rice. Cook for another 2-3 minutes.
4. Pour the coconut milk, water, stock, ginger, and kosher salt.
5. Add the beans and thyme. Place the Scotch bonnet or whole habanero chili and stir gently.
6. Bring to a boil. Over low heat, cover and simmer until rice is cooked through, about 15-20 minutes.
7. Remove from the heat and use a fork to fluff the rice.
8. Remove the chili and serve with some lime wedges.

Nutrition: Calories: 876; Carbohydrates 292 g; Protein 51 g; Fat 41 g; Sodium 574 mg

54. BLACK BEAN QUINOA

Preparation Time: 10 minutes   **Cooking Time:** 30 minutes   **Servings:** 4

INGREDIENTS

- 1 teaspoon olive oil
- 1 onion, chopped
- 3 garlic cloves, chopped
- ¾ cup quinoa, uncooked
- 1 ½ cup vegetable broth
- 1 teaspoon ground cumin
- ½ teaspoon cayenne pepper
- Sea salt and black pepper, to taste
- 1 cup frozen corn kernels
- 2 cans black beans, rinsed and drained

DIRECTIONS

1. Place a pan over medium heat and add the olive oil.
2. Cook the onion and garlic in the oil for 4 minutes.
3. Add the quinoa to the pan and mix well with the onion and garlic. Pour in the broth, then season with the spices and mix well.
4. Bring to a boil, reduce the heat to low then cover and let simmer for 20 minutes.
5. Stir in the corn and black beans to the pan, then cook for another 5 minutes.
6. Season with more salt and pepper to taste.

Nutrition: Calories: 876; Carbohydrates 236 g; Protein 36 g; Fat 27 g

55. TURKEY THREE BEAN CHILI

Preparation Time: 10 minutes   **Cooking Time:** 60 minutes   **Servings:** 4

INGREDIENTS

- 1 (20 ounces) package ground turkey, 93% lean
- 1 (4.5 ounces) can green chiles, chopped
- 1 (28 ounces) can fire-roasted diced tomatoes with their juices
- 1 (16 ounces) can tomato sauce
- 1 small onion, chopped
- 2 tablespoons chili powder
- 1 (15 ounces) can pinto beans, drained and rinsed; or 5 ounces dry pinto beans, soaked and cooked
- 1 (15 ounces) can kidney beans, drained and rinsed; or 5 ounces dry kidney beans, soaked and cooked
- 1 (15 ounces) can black beans, drained and rinsed; or 5 ounces dry black beans, soaked and cooked
- 1 tablespoon garlic, minced
- 1 teaspoon dried oregano
- Pinch ground cumin
- Cooking spray

DIRECTIONS

1. Spray a large deep saucepan or skillet with cooking spray and heat over medium heat.
2. Add the turkey and cook until evenly browned about 8-10 minutes.
3. In a slow cooker, add the ground turkey, green chilies, diced tomatoes, tomato sauce, onion, chili powder, garlic, all the beans, oregano, and ground cumin. Stir until well combined.
4. Close the lid and ensure it's in the sealing position. Select the HIGH setting and set the timer for 4 hours (if cooking using the LOW mode, set a timer for 7 hours).
5. When done, serve warm.

Nutrition: Calories: 1659; Carbohydrates 289 g; Protein 60 g; Fat 55 g; Sodium 877 mg

56. AVOCADO AND PINTO SALAD

Preparation Time: 10 minutes   **Cooking Time:** 0 minutes   **Servings:** 4

INGREDIENTS

- 2 cups pinto beans, cooked
- 2 large tomatoes, chopped
- ¼ cup chopped cilantro
- 2 scallions, thinly sliced
- 3 tablespoons lime juice
- ¼ cup balsamic vinegar
- 1 avocado, stone removed, peeled, and chopped into chunks
- Sea salt and ground black pepper, to taste

DIRECTIONS

1. Add the pinto beans and balsamic vinegar to a large mixing bowl. Toss and then leave to sit for 60 minutes. Stir occasionally.
2. Add the remaining ingredients, and gently toss everything together.

Nutrition: Calories: 986; Carbohydrates 106 g; Protein 27 g; Fat 47 g

57. RICE, BEAN, AND SAUSAGE MEAL

Preparation Time: 10 minutes   **Cooking Time:** 40 minutes   **Servings:** 4

INGREDIENTS

- 1 cup basmati rice
- 1 tablespoon vegetable oil
- 1 (12.8 ounces) package smoked Andouille sausage, thinly sliced
- 1 medium sweet onion, diced
- 1 green bell pepper, cored and diced
- 2 stalks celery, diced
- 3 garlic cloves, minced
- 2 tablespoons tomato paste
- 1 ½ teaspoon no-salt-added Cajun seasoning
- 1 teaspoon hot sauce
- 3 cups low-sodium chicken stock
- 1 bay leaf
- 3 (15 ounces) cans red beans, drained and rinsed; or 15 ounces dry red beans, soaked and cooked
- Kosher salt and freshly ground black pepper, to taste
- 2 tablespoons flat-leaf parsley, chopped

DIRECTIONS

1. In a large saucepan, cook the rice with 2 cups of water over medium-high heat per package instructions.
2. Once the rice is cooked through, drain, and set aside.
3. In a large stockpot/Dutch oven, heat oil over medium heat.
4. Add the sausage and cook for 3-4 minutes or until evenly browned. Set aside to drain on a plate lined with a paper towel.
5. Add the bell pepper, onion, and celery. Cook until tender, about 3-4 minutes.
6. Add the garlic, tomato paste, and Cajun seasoning. Cook for 1 minute or until fragrant.
7. Add the hot sauce, stock, bay leaf, beans, and sausage. Season with freshly ground black pepper and salt to taste.
8. Bring to a boil. Over low heat, cover, and simmer for about 15 minutes.
9. Remove the cover and simmer until the mixture thickens, about another 15 minutes.
10. Mash the beans slightly, optional, then season with freshly ground black pepper and kosher salt to taste. Top with parsley.
11. Serve warm with the cooked rice.

Nutrition: Calories: 497; Carbohydrates 237 g; Protein 38 g; Fat 30 g; Sodium 884 mg

58. PUMPKIN BACON BEAN STEW

Preparation Time: 10 minutes   **Cooking Time:** 30 minutes   **Servings:** 4

INGREDIENTS

- 1 pound dried cranberry or pinto beans, soaked and cooked
- 2 tablespoons vegetable oil
- ½ pound smoked bacon, diced into small pieces
- 4 large garlic cloves, minced
- 1 large white onion, cut into ½-inch slices
- 1 green bell pepper, cored and cut into ½-inch slices
- 1 jalapeno pepper, seeded and minced
- 2 teaspoons ground cumin
- 1 teaspoon dried oregano
- 1 teaspoon sweet paprika
- Freshly ground black pepper and kosher salt, to taste
- 4 plum tomatoes, coarsely chopped
- 6 cups low-sodium chicken stock (or preferred)
- ½ pound pumpkin or butternut squash, peeled, seeded, and cut into 1-inch chunks
- 1 ¼ cup corn
- 2 tablespoons fresh basil, coarsely chopped

DIRECTIONS

1. In a large and deep saucepan/skillet, heat oil over medium heat.
2. Add the bacon and cook until evenly crisped and browned, about 4-5 minutes.
3. Add the garlic and cook until fragrant, about 1 minute.
4. Add the bell pepper, jalapeno pepper, onion, oregano, ground cumin, 1 teaspoon freshly ground black pepper, 1 teaspoon kosher salt, and paprika. Cook until vegetables soften, about 4-5 minutes.
5. Add the tomatoes and cook for 2 minutes or until softened.
6. Add the stock and beans, then bring them to a boil.
7. Over low heat, partially cover and simmer for about 45 minutes, stirring occasionally.
8. Add the pumpkin/squash and cook for about 15 minutes or until tender.
9. Mix in the corn and basil, then simmer for 10 minutes more over medium heat.
10. Season to taste with freshly ground black pepper and kosher salt.
11. Serve warm.

Nutrition: Calories: 1293; Carbohydrates 267 g; Protein 66 g; Fat 45 g; Sodium 435 mg

59. CHORIZO AND BEAN STEW

Preparation Time: 10 minutes   **Cooking Time:** 30 minutes   **Servings:** 4

INGREDIENTS

- 1 tablespoon olive oil
- 7 ounces chorizo sausage, thickly sliced
- 1 yellow onion, chopped
- 14 ounces boneless, skinless chicken breasts, cubed
- 1 medium red tomato, roughly chopped
- 1 (14 ounces) can cannellini beans, drained and rinsed; or 5 ounces dry cannellini beans, soaked and cooked
- 1 large potato, cut into small cubes
- 2 cups low-sodium chicken stock
- 4 tablespoons flat-leaf parsley, chopped

DIRECTIONS

1. In a medium to large deep saucepan, heat oil over medium heat.
2. Add the onion, chorizo, and chicken. Cook for 4-5 minutes.
3. Add the tomato and cook for 2-3 minutes or until softened.
4. Add the stock, beans, and potato. Stir gently to combine, then bring to a boil.
5. Over low heat, simmer until chicken is cooked through and potatoes are tender for about 20 minutes.
6. Top with the parsley and serve warm.

Nutrition: Calories: 933; Carbohydrates 185 g; Protein 73 g; Fat 41 g; Sodium 3042 mg

60. WARM CHICKEN BALSAMIC SALAD

Preparation Time: 10 minutes   **Cooking Time:** 0 minutes   **Servings:** 4

INGREDIENTS

- 2 chicken breasts, cut into thin strips
- 2 garlic cloves, minced
- 2 tablespoons wholegrain mustard
- 2 tablespoons balsamic vinegar
- 1 tablespoon olive oil
- 1 can cannellini beans, drained and rinsed
- 1 cup cherry tomatoes, halved
- 1 red onion, chopped
- 1 red bell pepper, chopped
- ½ cup feta cheese, crumbled
- 2 pressed cups rocket leaves

DIRECTIONS

1. Place a pan over medium heat and add the olive oil.
2. Once the oil is heated add the garlic and chicken. Cook the chicken in the garlic, stirring frequently, for 3 minutes.
3. Add the balsamic vinegar, onion, pepper, tomatoes, and beans. Mix everything to coat well and then cook for a further 4 minutes, or until the chicken is cooked through.
4. Take off the heat and add the mustard, toss well to ensure everything is well mixed.
5. In a large serving bowl add the cheese and rocket. Toss well to mix.
6. Pour the contents of the pan, along with any juices, directly into the mixing bowl and toss well.

Nutrition: Calories: 766; Carbohydrates 112 g; Protein 65 g; Fat 47 g

61. SOUTH-WESTERN CHICKEN BEAN SALAD

Preparation Time: 10 minutes   **Cooking Time:** 0 minutes   **Servings:** 4

INGREDIENTS

- 2 chicken breasts, cooked, cooled, and cut into small pieces
- 1 can black beans, rinsed and drained
- 1 cup frozen corn, defrosted
- 2 scallions, chopped
- ½ red bell pepper, chopped
- ½ green bell pepper, chopped
- 2 tablespoons lime juice
- 1 tablespoon olive oil
- 2 tablespoons taco or fajita seasoning
- ¼ cup sour cream
- ¼ cup salsa

DIRECTIONS

1. Add all the ingredients, except the sour cream, to a large mixing bowl. Toss everything together to mix well. A good tip is to add 1 teaspoon of taco seasoning at a time before tossing. This will ensure it is evenly distributed.
2. Drizzle the sour cream evenly over the salad.

Nutrition: Calories: 452; Carbohydrates 136 g; Protein 77 g; Fat 15 g

62. LAMB BEAN STEW

Preparation Time: 10 minutes   **Cooking Time:** 30 minutes   **Servings:** 4

INGREDIENTS

- 2 pounds lamb stew meat, cut into bite-sized pieces
- 2 cups white onion, finely diced
- 1 ½ cup celery, finely diced
- 2½ cups carrots, peeled and finely diced
- 4 garlic cloves, minced
- 1 tablespoon fresh rosemary, minced
- 1 tablespoon fresh thyme, leaves only, minced
- 1 pound Great Northern beans, soaked and cooked
- 4 cups low-sodium chicken stock
- 1 ½ teaspoon kosher salt, divided
- 1 ½ teaspoon freshly ground black pepper, divided
- ½ cup all-purpose flour
- ½ teaspoon ground coriander

DIRECTIONS

1. In a large mixing bowl, add the flour, ½ teaspoon freshly ground black pepper, ½ teaspoon kosher salt, and ground coriander. Combine well.
2. Add the lamb pieces and toss to coat well.
3. In a medium to large stockpot/Dutch oven, heat oil over medium heat.
4. Add the lamb pieces and cook until evenly browned.
5. Place the onion, garlic, and celery. Cook until softened and translucent, about 3-5 minutes.
6. Add the rosemary, thyme, stock, beans, 1 teaspoon of kosher salt, and 1 teaspoon of freshly ground black pepper. Bring to a boil.
7. Over low heat, add the carrots and simmer until meat is cooked through, about 2 hours while stirring occasionally.
8. Season to taste with more freshly ground black pepper and kosher salt.
9. Serve warm.

Nutrition: Calories: 1956; Carbohydrates 235 g; Protein 94 g; Fat 69 g; Sodium 1038 mg

63. APRICOT CHICKPEA STEW

Preparation Time: 10 minutes　　　**Cooking Time:** 30 minutes　　　**Servings:** 4

INGREDIENTS

- ¼ cup low-sodium vegetable broth
- 1 small sweet white onion, chopped
- 1 bell pepper, cored and diced
- 1 leek, rinsed and sliced into ¼-inch rounds
- 3-4 medium carrots, peeled and sliced
- 1 (15 ounces) can garbanzo beans, drained and rinsed; or 5 ounces dry garbanzo beans, soaked and cooked
- ¼ teaspoon garlic powder
- 2 teaspoons curry powder
- 2 teaspoons ground cumin
- 1½ teaspoons sweet paprika
- ½ teaspoon ground turmeric
- ⅛ teaspoon ground ginger
- Pinch ground cinnamon
- 2½ cups low-sodium vegetable broth
- ½ cup packed dried apricots, roughly chopped or whole
- ¼ cup black olives, pitted and sliced
- Handful cilantro, roughly chopped
- Cooked quinoa or cooked grain preferred, to serve

DIRECTIONS

1. In a medium to large stockpot/deep saucepan/Dutch oven, add a splash of broth and heat it over medium heat.
2. Add the onion, leek, and bell pepper. Cook until softened and translucent, about 4-5 minutes.
3. Add the carrots, beans, garlic powder, and all the spices. Combine well and cook for 1 minute.
4. Add the black olives, broth, and dried apricots. Stir gently, then bring to a boil.
5. Over low heat, cover and simmer for about 20 minutes or until vegetables are tender.
6. Top with some cilantro. Serve warm with cooked quinoa or your choice of cooked grain.

Nutrition: Calories: 824; Carbohydrates 123 g; Protein 50 g; Fat 19 g; Sodium 791 mg

64. BLACK BEAN VEGGIE STEW

Preparation Time: 10 minutes   **Cooking Time:** 50 minutes   **Servings:** 4

INGREDIENTS

- 1 tablespoon olive oil
- ½ cup red bell pepper, cored and chopped
- 2 large onions, chopped
- ½ cup celery, chopped
- ½ cup carrot, peeled and chopped
- ¼ cup dry sherry or low-sodium chicken broth
- 2 tablespoons garlic, minced
- 1 (14.5 ounces) can diced tomatoes with their juices
- 2 tablespoons tomato paste
- 2 (15 ounces) cans black beans, drained and rinsed; or 15 ounces dry black beans, soaked and cooked
- 1 (14.5 ounces) container low-sodium chicken broth
- 2 tablespoons honey
- 2 teaspoons ground cumin
- 4 teaspoons chili powder
- ½ teaspoon dried oregano
- ¼ cup cilantro, minced
- 5 tablespoons Monterey Jack cheese, shredded
- 5 tablespoons low-fat sour cream
- 2 tablespoons green onion, chopped

DIRECTIONS

1. In a medium to large Dutch oven, heat oil and sherry over medium heat.
2. Add the onions, red bell pepper, carrot, and celery. Cook until softened and translucent.
3. Place the garlic and cook until fragrant, about 1 minute.
4. Pour the tomatoes, tomato paste, beans, broth, honey, ground cumin, chili powder, and oregano. Bring to a boil.
5. Over low heat, cover, and simmer for about 40 minutes.
6. Add the cilantro and simmer until the stew is thickened about 10-15 minutes.
7. Garnish with sour cream, Monterey Jack cheese, and chopped green onions.
8. Serve warm.

Nutrition: Calories: 795; Carbohydrates 161 g; Protein 69 g; Fat 52; Sodium 922 mg

65. BUTTER BEAN DIP

Preparation Time: 7 minutes   **Cooking Time:** 10 minutes   **Servings:** 4

INGREDIENTS

- 1 can butter beans, drained
- 1 garlic clove, peeled
- 5 tablespoons extra-virgin olive oil
- 1 lemon, juiced
- Handful basil leaves, chopped
- ½ teaspoon chili flakes

DIRECTIONS

1. Blend all ingredients in a food processor until smooth.
2. Place in a bowl and serve with chips or toast.

Nutrition: Calories: 236; Carbohydrates 65 g; Protein 18 g; Fat 8 g; Sodium 870 mg

66. BACON BEAN SANDWICHES

Preparation Time: 7 minutes   **Cooking Time:** 25 minutes   **Servings:** 4

INGREDIENTS

- 1 can baked beans
- 5 slices bread, lightly toasted
- 10 bacon strips, cooked and drained
- 1 large white onion, sliced into rings
- 5 slices American cheese

DIRECTIONS

1. Place toast on a baking sheet.
2. Spoon beans on top of bread slices.
3. Top with bacon, onion rings, and a cheese slice.
4. Bake for 15-20 minutes at 350°F or until cheese melts and turns brown.

Nutrition: Calories: 846; Carbohydrates 161 g; Protein 48 g; Fat 37 g; Sodium 456 mg

67. BLACK BEAN BURGER PATTIES

Preparation Time: 7 minutes   **Cooking Time:** 33 minutes   **Servings:** 4

INGREDIENTS

- 1 can black beans, drained
- 3 garlic cloves, peeled
- ½ onion, chopped
- ½ green bell pepper, chopped
- 1 egg, beaten
- 1 tablespoon chili powder
- 1 tablespoon cumin
- ½ cup bread crumbs

DIRECTIONS

1. In a food processor, mash beans, bell pepper, onion, garlic egg, chili powder, and cumin together.
2. Mix in breadcrumbs until you get a thick paste consistency. Fry in a pan as you would a normal burger.

Nutrition: Calories: 567; Carbohydrates 48 g; Protein 65 g; Fat 33 g; Sodium 277 mg

68. WHITE BEAN FRITTERS

Preparation Time: 7 minutes   **Cooking Time:** 33 minutes   **Servings:** 4

INGREDIENTS

- 1 can white beans, drained
- 2 garlic cloves, chopped
- 1 small onion, chopped
- 1 parsley sprig, chopped
- 1 tablespoon white flour
- Salt and pepper
- 5 tablespoons olive oil

DIRECTIONS

1. Place beans, garlic, onions, and parsley in a food processor and blend until smooth.
2. Season with salt and pepper to taste.
3. Add flour and mix.
4. Form into fritters and fry in hot olive oil.

Nutrition: Calories: 348; Carbohydrates 76 g; Protein 25 g; Fat 15 g; Sodium 572 mg

69. BAKED BEAN FRITTERS

Preparation Time: 7 minutes   **Cooking Time:** 25 minutes   **Servings:** 4

INGREDIENTS

- 1 can baked beans in tomato sauce, drained, reserve sauce
- 1 cup self-raising flour
- 3 tablespoons milk
- 2 eggs, beaten
- 1 teaspoon mild curry
- 5 tablespoons olive oil

DIRECTIONS

1. Blend beans, flour, milk, eggs, and curry powder in a food processor.
2. Fry fritters in hot oil until golden brown.
3. Serve with tomato sauce.

Nutrition: Calories: 365; Carbohydrates 19 g; Protein 56 g; Fat 46 g; Sodium 515 mg

70. SIMPLE BEAN BURGER

Preparation Time: 7 minutes   **Cooking Time:** 25 minutes   **Servings:** 4

INGREDIENTS

- 2 cans pinto beans, drained
- ½ teaspoon garlic powder
- 2 large eggs, beaten
- 1 cup dried breadcrumbs
- Salt and pepper to taste
- 4 pieces hamburger buns

DIRECTIONS

1. Mash beans and add breadcrumbs, eggs, pepper, and garlic powder.
2. Shape into patties and fry or grill according to your preference.
3. Serve warm on hamburger buns.

Nutrition: Calories: 876; Carbohydrates 116 g; Protein 69 g; Fat 37 g; Sodium 471 mg

71. EASY FALAFELS

Preparation Time: 7 minutes   **Cooking Time:** 33 minutes   **Servings:** 4

INGREDIENTS

- 1 can chickpeas, drained
- 1 medium onion, chopped
- 1 egg, beaten
- 2 tablespoons dried parsley
- 1 tablespoon garlic powder
- 1 tablespoon curry powder
- ½ teaspoon black pepper, ground
- 1 tablespoon lemon juice
- ¼ cup breadcrumbs
- 5 tablespoons olive oil

DIRECTIONS

1. Blend chickpeas, onion, parsley, curry powder, garlic powder, egg, lemon juice, and black pepper.
2. Roll into balls and fry in hot oil.
3. Serve with pita bread and plain yogurt.

Nutrition: Calories: 437; Carbohydrates 128 g; Protein 67 g; Fat 38 g; Sodium 212 mg

72. BLACK BEAN AVOCADO BROWNIE

Preparation Time: 10 minutes   **Cooking Time:** 30 minutes   **Servings:** 4

INGREDIENTS

- 1 (15 ounces) can black beans, drained and rinsed; or 5 ounces dry black beans, soaked and cooked
- ½ cup unsweetened cocoa powder
- 3 large eggs
- ¼ cup vegetable oil or melted coconut oil
- ¾ cup granulated sugar
- ¼ teaspoon kosher salt
- 1 teaspoon baking powder
- 1 teaspoon pure vanilla extract
- 1 medium avocado, pitted and peeled
- 1 cup dark chocolate chips
- Cooking spray

DIRECTIONS

1. Preheat oven to 350°F (175°C). Grease an 8x8 baking dish with cooking spray or cooking oil.
2. In a food processor or blender, add all the ingredients except the chocolate chips. Blend on pulse mode until you get a smooth, rich mixture.
3. Add the brownie mixture to the baking dish and top with the chocolate chips.
4. Bake for about 35-40 minutes or until a toothpick comes out clean.
5. Let cool for 10-15 minutes.
6. Slice and serve warm. To store, refrigerate in an airtight container for 4-5 days.

Nutrition: Calories: 912; Carbohydrates 82 g; Protein 57 g; Fat 55 g; Sodium 193 mg

73. WHITE NAVY BEAN CARROT BLONDIES

Preparation Time: 10 minutes   **Cooking Time:** 30 minutes   **Servings:** 4

INGREDIENTS

- ½ cup old-fashioned oats
- ¼ cup creamy peanut butter
- ¼ teaspoon kosher salt
- ½ teaspoon baking powder
- ½ cup maple syrup
- 1 teaspoon pure vanilla extract
- 1 (15.5 ounces) can white navy beans, drained and rinsed; or 5 ounces dry white navy beans, soaked and cooked
- 1 cup carrots, peeled and shredded
- ¼ cup chocolate chips
- Cooking spray

DIRECTIONS

1. Preheat oven to 350°F (175°C). Grease an 8x8 pie pan or baking dish with cooking spray or cooking oil.
2. In a food processor or blender, add the oats. Blend on pulse mode to make flour out of the oats.
3. Add the peanut butter, kosher salt, baking powder, maple syrup, vanilla extract, beans, and carrots to the blender.
4. Blend on pulse mode until you get a smooth, rich mixture.
5. Add the mixture to the pie pan/baking dish, then top with the remaining chocolate chips. You can also add more shredded carrots on top if desired.
6. Bake until the edges start to brown, about 20-25 minutes.
7. Let cool for 10-15 minutes.
8. Slice into squares and serve warm. To store, refrigerate for up to 5-7 days in an air-tight container.

Nutrition: Calories: 1165; Carbohydrates 80 g; Protein 47 g; Fat 35 g,; Sodium 114 mg

74. GARBANZO BEAN CHOCOLATE CAKE

Preparation Time: 10 minutes   **Cooking Time:** 40 minutes   **Servings:** 4

INGREDIENTS

- 1 ½ cup semisweet chocolate chips
- 1 (19 ounces) can garbanzo beans, drained and rinsed; or 6 ounces dry garbanzo beans, soaked and cooked
- 4 large eggs
- ¾ cup granulated sugar
- ½ teaspoon baking powder
- 1 tablespoon confectioner's sugar
- Cooking spray

DIRECTIONS

1. Preheat an oven to 350°F (175°C). Grease a 9-inch round cake pan or baking dish with cooking spray or cooking oil.
2. Melt the chocolate in a microwave over medium-high heat in an oven-safe bowl or container. Melt for 2 minutes while stirring regularly.
3. In a food processor or blender, add the eggs and beans. Blend on pulse mode until you get a smooth, rich mixture.
4. Add the baking powder and sugar. Blend again.
5. Add the melted chocolate and blend until smooth.
6. Add the cake mix to the cake pan/baking dish. Bake for about 40 minutes or until a toothpick comes out clean.
7. Let cool for 10-15 minutes.
8. Dust with the confectioner's sugar, slice and serve warm.

Nutrition: Calories: 1127; Carbohydrates 182 g; Protein 57 g; Fat 50; Sodium 180 mg

75. BLACK BEAN CHOCO TRUFFLES

Preparation Time: 10 minutes   **Cooking Time:** 30 minutes   **Servings:** 4

INGREDIENTS

Truffles:
- ¼ cup unsweetened cocoa powder
- ½ teaspoon pure vanilla extract
- 1 (15 ounces) can black beans, drained and rinsed; or 5 ounces dry black beans, soaked and cooked
- 1 ripe medium avocado, pitted and peeled
- ½ cup dark chocolate chips
- ½ teaspoon coconut oil

Chocolate Coating:
- 1 cup dark chocolate chips
- 1 teaspoon coconut oil
- Sea salt, to taste
- Shredded coconut (optional)

DIRECTIONS

For Truffles:
1. In a food processor or blender, add vanilla extract, cocoa powder, beans, and avocado.
2. Blend on pulse mode until you get a smooth, rich mixture.
3. Melt the chocolate chips and coconut oil in a microwave over medium-high heat in an oven-safe bowl or container. Melt for 2 minutes while stirring regularly.
4. Add the melted chocolate to the bean mixture. Mix until well combined.
5. Add the mixture to a large bowl and refrigerate until the batter firms up, about 10-20 minutes.
6. Prepare truffle balls from the mixture (about 1-2 tablespoons of batter per truffle).
7. Arrange the truffles on a baking sheet lined with parchment paper. Refrigerate until well set.

For the Chocolate Coating:
8. Melt the chocolate chips and coconut oil in a microwave over medium-high heat in an oven-safe bowl or container. Melt for 2 minutes while stirring regularly.
9. Roll the truffles into the melted chocolate until covered evenly and arrange them over a baking sheet lined with parchment paper.
10. Sprinkle the sea salt and shredded coconut, optional on top. Refrigerate for 5 minutes more.
11. Serve chilled.

Nutrition: Calories: 1233; Carbohydrates 161 g; Protein 32 g; Fat 26 g; Sodium 73 mg

76. CHOCOLATE AND PEANUT BUTTER BITES

Preparation Time: 10 minutes   **Cooking Time:** 30 minutes   **Servings:** 4

INGREDIENTS

Dough:
- 1 (15.5 ounces) can chickpeas, drained and rinsed; or 5 ounces dry chickpeas, soaked and cooked
- 1 teaspoon pure vanilla extract
- 3 tablespoons maple syrup
- 1 tablespoon vegetable oil
- 2 tablespoons peanut butter powder
- ½ cup peanut butter, smooth or chunky
- ¼ teaspoon kosher salt
- ¼ cup chocolate chips

Drizzle:
- ¼ cup chocolate chips
- ½ teaspoon coconut oil
- ¼ teaspoon sea salt (optional)

DIRECTIONS

1. Line a baking sheet with parchment paper.
2. In a food processor or blender, add the chickpeas. Blend on pulse mode until chickpeas are broken down.
3. Add the vanilla extract, maple syrup, oil, powdered peanut butter, peanut butter, vanilla, and salt to the blender. Pulse for about 1 minute until smooth.
4. Add the batter to a bowl and mix in the chocolate chips.
5. Refrigerate for 5 minutes or until the batter firms up.
6. Roll into balls of around 1 inch.
7. Transfer to the prepared baking sheet.

For the Chocolate Drizzle:

8. Melt the chocolate chips and coconut oil in a microwave over medium-high heat in an oven-safe bowl or container. Melt for 2 minutes while stirring regularly.
9. Drizzle the sauce over the prepared dough bites. Sprinkle sea salt on top, if desired.
10. Refrigerate for 5 minutes more, then serve chilled.

Nutrition: Calories: 625; Carbohydrates 298 g; Protein 28 g; Fat 68 g; Sodium 208 mg

CHAPTER 4
DAILY RICE RECIPES

77. JAMAICAN BEANS AND RICE

Preparation Time: 5 minutes   **Cooking Time:** 22 minutes   **Servings:** 10

INGREDIENTS

- 1 ½ cup canned red kidney beans, rinsed and drained
- ¼ cup minced onion
- 2 cups long-grain rice
- 2 ¼ cups water
- 1 ¾ cup coconut milk
- 1 scallion, chopped
- 1 garlic clove, crushed
- 1 fresh thyme sprig
- 1 teaspoon coconut oil
- 1 whole scotch bonnet hot pepper, not chopped
- Salt and ground pepper to taste

DIRECTIONS

1. Heat the olive oil in a medium-sized saucepan over medium heat. Add the scallion, onion, garlic, and thyme. Sauté for a few minutes, until the onions are translucent and lightly browned.
2. Stir in the rice and beans. Pour in the coconut milk and water and season with salt and pepper. Add the whole scotch bonnet pepper, stir to combine, and bring to a boil.
3. When it starts boiling, remove the pepper and cook until the rice is tender and almost all the liquid has been absorbed.
4. Cover the saucepan, reduce the heat and let it simmer for about 25 minutes. Remove the saucepan from the heat and let it rest covered for 10 minutes so that the steam will finish cooking the rice.
5. Serve hot.

Nutrition: Calories: 659; Carbohydrates 134 g; Protein 37 g; Fat 43 g; Sugar 0.1 g; Sodium 108 mg

78. LIME RICE AND AVOCADO BLACK BEANS

Preparation Time: 7 minutes   **Cooking Time:** 33 minutes   **Servings:** 4

INGREDIENTS

For Beans:
- 3 cups canned black beans, drained and rinsed
- 1 cup vegetable broth
- 1 ½ cup water
- 2 garlic cloves, minced
- ½ small onion, minced
- 1 tablespoon extra-virgin olive oil
- ¼ teaspoon cumin
- 2 teaspoons chili powder
- Salt and pepper, to taste
- 1 avocado, peeled and sliced

For the Lime Rice:
- 3 cups water
- 1 cup long-grain white rice
- 3 tablespoons chopped cilantro
- ½ teaspoon salt
- 1 tablespoon canola oil
- ½ lime, juiced

DIRECTIONS

For Beans:

1. Heat the oil in a large pot over medium heat. Add the onion, season with pepper and salt, and fry for about 10 minutes, until soft. Add the minced garlic and sauté for about 30 seconds, stirring continuously. Add the cumin and chili powder and cook for 30 seconds.
2. Add the drained beans, pour in the water and vegetable broth, and bring to a boil. Turn the heat down and let the soup simmer for 15 minutes.
3. Scoop 2 ladles of soup into a food processor or blender and pulse until the mixture becomes smooth. Return the mixture to the pot and stir well.

For the Lime Rice:

4. In a saucepan, pour the water, oil, and salt and bring to a boil. Add the rice, turn the heat down, cover the pot, and let it simmer for about 15 minutes, until the rice gets tender. Fluff the rice with a fork and add the chopped cilantro and lime juice. Stir well.
5. When serving, divide the hot rice into bowls and top with the hot beans and avocado slices.

Nutrition: Calories: 1132; Carbohydrates 169 g; Protein 48 g; Fat 38 g; Sodium 118 mg

79. BAJA BLACK BEANS AND RICE WITH CORN

Preparation Time: 7 minutes   **Cooking Time:** 43 minutes   **Servings:** 6

INGREDIENTS

- 2 cups brown rice
- 1 ½ cup canned corn, drained
- 1 ½ cup black beans, rinsed and drained
- ½ cup chopped cilantro
- ½ cup chopped red onion
- 4 fresh tomatoes, diced
- 1 jalapeno pepper, seeded and diced
- 1 tablespoon olive oil
- 2 tablespoons fresh lime juice
- ¼ teaspoon fresh ground pepper
- ½ teaspoon salt

DIRECTIONS

1. Place the rice in a saucepan, pour in cold water to cover the rice by a few inches, and bring it to a boil. Reduce the heat, cover the pot and let it simmer for 20-25 minutes, until the rice is tender.
2. In a medium bowl, combine all the ingredients and mix well.
3. When the rice is done, divide it into plates and top with a big scoop of the black bean mixture.

Nutrition: Calories: 842; Fat 8 g; Carbohydrates 166 g; Protein 34 g; Sodium 950 mg

80. BROWN RICE AND GARBANZO BEANS WITH ASPARAGUS

Preparation Time: 7 minutes   **Cooking Time:** 43 minutes   **Servings:** 6

INGREDIENTS

- 1 cup brown rice
- 1 cup slivered almonds, toasted
- 1 ½ cup canned garbanzo beans, drained and dried
- Bunch asparagus, cut into 1-inch pieces
- 2 garlic cloves, smashed and chopped
- 1 medium yellow onion, chopped
- 3 tablespoons extra-virgin olive oil
- 1 teaspoon kosher salt

For the Dressing:
- 1/3 cup tahini
- 2 tablespoons lemon juice, freshly squeezed
- 1 teaspoon lemon zest
- 2 tablespoons hot water
- 2 garlic cloves, smashed and chopped
- 2 teaspoons kosher salt
- 3 tablespoons extra-virgin olive oil

DIRECTIONS

1. Cook the rice until tender according to the package directions.
2. In the meantime, in a small bowl, whisk the lemon zest, chopped garlic, tahini, lemon juice, and olive oil. Season with salt and pour in the hot water. Mix and set aside.
3. Heat the olive oil in a big skillet over medium-high heat. Add the dried garbanzo beans and a pinch of salt. Sauté the beans for just a couple of minutes until they form a little crust. Add the onions and garlic and sauté for a minute.
4. Stir in the asparagus pieces, add a pinch of salt, and cover the skillet for just 1 minute until the steam softens the asparagus.
5. Add the rice and almond slivers, reserving a few for garnish.
6. Taste for flavor and adjust the seasonings if necessary. Drizzle with the dressing and serve warm.

Nutrition: Calories: 1268; Carbohydrates 143 g; Protein 48 g; Fat 73 g; Sugar 16 g; Sodium418 mg

81. COLORFUL RICE AND BLACK BEANS BOWL

Preparation Time: 3 minutes   **Cooking Time:** 24 minutes   **Servings:** 4-6

INGREDIENTS

- 1 cup red quinoa
- 1 cup long-grain brown rice
- 2 cups vegetable broth
- ½ cup cilantro
- 1 ½ cup canned black beans, drained and well-rinsed
- 2 cups frozen corn
- 1 small onion, finely diced
- 2 garlic cloves, minced
- 1 red bell pepper, finely diced
- 3 carrots, chopped or shredded
- 2 tablespoons coconut oil
- ¼ teaspoon cayenne pepper
- 2 teaspoons ground cumin
- 2 limes, juiced
- Salt and pepper, to taste

DIRECTIONS

1. First, prepare the rice by placing it in a medium saucepan. Pour enough water to cover the rice for about 2 inches. Cover the saucepan and cook for about 40 minutes, until the rice is tender. Drain and keep covered in the saucepan.
2. In a small saucepan, combine the quinoa and vegetable broth and bring to a boil. Let it simmer for 20 minutes, until the broth has been absorbed and the quinoa is tender.
3. Heat the coconut oil in a large skillet. Add the chopped onion, season with pepper, and sauté for about 5 minutes, or until the onion is lightly browned. Add the garlic and cook for about 30 seconds, until fragrant. Mix in the carrots. If you do not want the carrots to be crunchy, add them earlier. Season with salt, pepper, cayenne, and cumin.
4. Add the cooked quinoa and rice to the mixture, then stir well. Mix in the black beans and frozen corn. Stir well to combine the vegetables and cook until heated through.
5. Top with lime juice and cilantro. Serve immediately.

Nutrition: Calories: 1230; Carbohydrates 225 g; Protein 43 g; Fat 25 g; Sodium 92 mg

82. FIESTA RICE AND BEANS

Preparation Time: 7 minutes   **Cooking Time:** 55 minutes   **Servings:** 4

INGREDIENTS

- 1 cup long-grain rice
- 2 cups water
- ¾ cup cooked corn, heated
- ¾ cup canned black beans, rinsed and heated
- 1 large scallion, diced
- 1 large tomato, diced
- 1 tablespoon freshly squeezed lime juice
- 2-4 tablespoons chopped cilantro
- Salt to taste

DIRECTIONS

1. In a medium saucepan, add the rice, pour 2 cups of water and bring to a boil. Reduce the heat and let it simmer for about 25 minutes, or until the rice becomes tender.
2. In a large bowl, combine the hot rice, heated beans, and corn, then stir well to combine the ingredients.
3. Add the diced tomato, scallion, and cilantro. Combine well. Season with salt and drizzle with lime juice.
4. Toss to combine the ingredients and serve.

Nutrition: Calories: 894; Carbohydrates 252 g; Protein 36 g; Fat 26 g; Sodium 168 mg

83. GREEK LENTILS AND RICE

Preparation Time: 7 minutes   **Cooking Time:** 60 minutes   **Servings:** 4

INGREDIENTS

- 1/3 cup white rice
- 2 cups water
- 1 cup dried lentils
- 1 garlic clove, minced
- 1 onion, minced
- 1 tablespoon tomato paste
- 4 tablespoons olive oil
- Salt and pepper to taste

DIRECTIONS

1. Place the lentils in a pot with plenty of water and bring them to a boil. Reduce the heat and cook until the lentils are tender. Drain well.
2. In a saucepan, heat the olive oil over medium heat, add the onion and garlic, then sauté until translucent. Stir in the rice and cooked lentils. Pour in 2 cups of water. Season to taste and add the tomato paste. Cook for 40-50 minutes.
3. Serve warm.

Nutrition: Calories: 785; Carbohydrates 116 g; Protein 28 g; Fat 21g; Sodium 300 mg

84. GREEN BEANS AND RICE WITH PUMPKIN

Preparation Time: 7 minutes   **Cooking Time:** 43 minutes   **Servings:** 4

INGREDIENTS

- 1 ½ cup white long-grain rice
- 4 cups vegetable stock
- ¾ cup green beans, topped, cut into 2-inch pieces
- 2 cups butternut pumpkin, deseeded, peeled, and cut into 1-inch pieces
- ¼ cup pine nuts
- 1 red onion, halved, thinly sliced
- ¼ cup fresh continental parsley leaves
- 1 teaspoon ground cumin
- 1 tablespoon olive oil

DIRECTIONS

1. In a large saucepan, combine the vegetable stock, rice, pumpkin, and cumin and bring to a boil. Cover the pan, reduce the heat and cook for about 12 minutes, or until the pumpkin and rice are tender.
2. 2 minutes before the end of cooking, add the beans. Remove from the heat and let them sit covered for 5 minutes.
3. Heat a frying pan over medium-high heat. Add the pine nuts and toast them for 2 minutes, stirring. When toasted, transfer them to a bowl.
4. In the same pan, heat the oil over medium heat. Add the onion and cook for 5 minutes, stirring occasionally, until browned. Remove from the heat.
5. Spoon the rice and pumpkin mixture into a serving bowl. Sprinkle with toasted nuts and top with the onions and parsley.

Nutrition: Calories: 1004; Carbohydrates 248 g; Protein 48 g; Fat 38 g; Sodium 175 mg

85. ASIAN RISOTTO

Preparation Time: 7 minutes   **Cooking Time:** 33 minutes   **Servings:** 4

INGREDIENTS

- ½ cup snake beans or thinly sliced green beans
- 1 ½ cup arborio risotto rice
- 3.5 ounces fresh shiitake mushrooms (optional)
- Buch coriander, leaves, and stalks separated, roughly chopped, divided
- 2 garlic cloves, chopped, divided
- 1 onion, sliced,
- 1 red chili, deseeded, finely chopped,
- 1 stem lemongrass, only white parts, finely chopped,
- 1 red capsicum, deseeded, finely sliced,
- 1 cup white wine
- 3 ½ cups vegetable stock
- 2 ½ tablespoons vegetable oil, divided
- 2 tablespoons ketjap manis
- 1 tablespoon grated fresh ginger,
- 1 lime, juiced
- ½ cup mixed Asian herbs (Vietnamese mint, Thai basil)

DIRECTIONS

1. In a deep frying pan, heat 1 ½ tablespoon of oil and add the onion, ginger, and 1 clove of garlic, chili, lemongrass, coriander stalks, and capsicum. Cook for about 1-2 minutes over medium heat. Stir in the rice, reduce the heat and cook for 1 minute more.
2. Pour in the white wine and cook until the liquid has evaporated. Gradually pour in the vegetable stock, stirring continuously. Cook until the liquid has been absorbed and the rice is tender.
3. Stir in the beans and cook for 2 minutes more. Remove from the heat, cover loosely and set aside.
4. Heat the remaining oil in a frying pan, add the remaining garlic and shiitake mushrooms and cook over high heat for about 2 minutes, until the shiitake begin to soften. Set aside.
5. Add the ketjap manis, coriander leaves, lime juice, and herbs to the rice and stir well to combine.
6. Serve warm in bowls garnished with sautéed shiitake.

Nutrition: Calories: 1300; Carbohydrates 250 g; Protein 27 g; Fat 12 g; Sodium 217 mg

86. RICE PILAF

Preparation Time: 10 minutes   **Cooking Time:** 50 minutes   **Servings:** 4

INGREDIENTS

- 2 tablespoons butter
- 1/2 cup orzo pasta
- 1/2 cup diced onion
- 2 garlic cloves, minced
- 1/2 cup uncooked white rice
- 2 cups chicken broth

DIRECTIONS

1. Melt the butter in a covered skillet over medium-low heat.
2. Cook and stir the orzo pasta until golden brown.
3. Stir in onion and cook until onion becomes translucent, then add garlic and cook for 1 minute.
4. Mix in the rice and chicken broth.
5. Increase heat to high and bring to a boil.
6. Reduce heat to medium-low, cover, and simmer until the rice is tender, and the liquid has been absorbed for about 20-25 minutes.
7. Remove from heat and let stand for 5 minutes, then fluff with a fork.

Nutrition: Calories: 654; Carbohydrates 97 g; Protein 19 g; Fat 23 g

87. RICE AND BEAN CASSEROLE

Preparation Time: 7 minutes   **Cooking Time:** 43 minutes   **Servings:** 4-6

INGREDIENTS

- 1 ½ cups brown rice
- 1 ½ cup (or 1 can) small red kidney beans
- 3 cups vegetable broth
- 1 ¾ cup canned organic tomato sauce
- 1 small white onion, finely chopped
- 2 cups frozen corn
- 2-3 handfuls baby spinach leaves, shredded
- 3 garlic cloves, minced
- 2 tablespoons extra-virgin olive oil
- 1 teaspoon chili powder
- 1 tablespoon cumin
- Sea salt and pepper to taste
- Fresh cilantro for garnish

DIRECTIONS

1. Preheat oven to 350°F. Lightly grease a baking dish (approximately 9x13 inches) and set aside.
2. In a large skillet, heat the olive oil over medium heat. Sauté the onions for a few minutes, until they are translucent and lightly golden. Stir in garlic and sauté until fragrant. Pour in the tomato sauce and add the chili powder, cumin pepper, and salt. Stir well and simmer for about 10 minutes.
3. In a large bowl, combine the uncooked brown rice, broth, beans, tomato mixture, and spinach. Stir well and transfer to the baking dish and top with the corn. Cover the baking dish with tin foil and bake for about 2 hours.
4. When the rice is tender, remove from the oven, top with fresh cilantro and serve warm.

Nutrition: Calories: 952; Carbohydrates 165 g; Protein 35 g; Fat 19 g; Sugar 0 g; Sodium 179 mg

88. FERMENTED YELLOW WAX BEANS

Preparation Time: 15 minutes   **Cooking Time:** 50 minutes   **Servings:** 1 quart

INGREDIENTS

- 4 cups yellow wax beans, fresh
- 1 ½ tablespoon non-iodized sea salt
- 2 cups filtered water

DIRECTIONS

1. In a large glass jar, dissolve the salt in the water. In another jar, add the beans. Pour the liquid on top of the beans, leaving at least a 1-inch head space.
2. Cover the jar with a top that is firmly secured. After 3 days, you will need to burp the jar by removing the lid just enough to hear the gasses discharge and then rapidly tightening it back up.
3. Set the jars in a place where they will not be disturbed and let them ferment for about 7-8 days. Put the jars in the refrigerator, where they will keep for months.

Nutrition: Calories: 1020; Carbohydrates 179g; Protein 65g; Fat 8g; Sodium 56 mg

89. STUFFED ACORN SQUASH WITH BEANS AND RICE

Preparation Time: 4 minutes | **Cooking Time:** 21 minutes | **Servings:** 4

INGREDIENTS

- ½ cup brown basmati rice
- 1 acorn squash, cleaned, halved
- 1 ½ cup canned black beans, drained and rinsed
- 1 medium onion, chopped
- 2 garlic cloves
- 1 cup sliced carrots
- 1 red pepper, chopped
- ½ cup chopped fresh cilantro
- 2 tablespoons olive oil
- 2 tablespoons agave nectar
- Handful raisins
- ¼ or ½ teaspoon turmeric
- Salt and pepper to taste

DIRECTIONS

1. Preheat the oven to 350°F.
2. Prepare the rice, by cooking it in a saucepan filled with water. When it starts boiling, reduce the heat and simmer until tender.
3. Drizzle the acorn squash halves with the agave nectar. Place them in a baking dish and roast for about 30 minutes until tender. Add a few tablespoons of water while roasting to retain moisture.
4. Heat the olive oil in a skillet over medium-high meat. Add the carrots, onions, garlic, red pepper, and raisins and fry until tender. Stir in the turmeric and cooked rice and mix well.
5. Add the chopped cilantro and black beans, then stir well to combine. Remove from the heat.
6. When the squash is done, you can drizzle it again with agave nectar, if desired, and then stuff it with the beans and rice mixture.
7. Return to the oven and cook for 10 minutes more if needed. Do not overcook it.
8. When done, cut the halves to get 4 pieces and serve.

Nutrition: Calories: 986; Carbohydrates 179 g; Protein 36 g; Fat 41 g; Sugar 0 g; Sodium 276 mg

90. THAI RICE AND GREEN BEANS

Preparation Time: 3 minutes | **Cooking Time:** 24 minutes | **Servings:** 4-6

INGREDIENTS

- 2 cups long-grain rice
- ½ cup fresh or frozen corn kernels
- 1 cup diced green beans
- 1 small onion, finely chopped
- 3 tablespoons coarsely chopped garlic
- 2 tablespoons vegetable oil
- ½ teaspoon fresh ground black pepper
- 2 teaspoons Thai green curry paste
- 2 tablespoons soy sauce

For Garnish:
- 1 lime, cut into wedges
- 1 cucumber, peeled, seeded, thinly sliced
- 3 scallions, sliced

DIRECTIONS

1. Prepare the rice by bringing a saucepan with water and rice to a boil. Reduce the heat and simmer for about 25 minutes, until the rice is tender. Spread the rice on a baking sheet to cool. Place in the fridge for at least 2 hours or overnight.
2. Heat a large frying pan and add the oil. When the oil is hot and begins to smoke slightly, add the onion, garlic, and black pepper. Cook for 2 minutes. Stir in the corn and green beans, then continue to stir-fry for about 3 minutes more.
3. Add the cold rice and fry for 5 minutes more. Stir in the curry paste and soy sauce. Cook for 2 minutes.
4. Serve warm and garnish with the cucumber, scallions, and lime.

Nutrition: Calories: 362; Carbohydrates 77 g; Protein 10 g; Fat 5 g; Sugar 4 g; Sodium 600 mg

91. EGYPTIAN RICE AND LENTILS

Preparation Time: 7 minutes   **Cooking Time:** 33 minutes   **Servings:** 4-6

INGREDIENTS

- 1 cup brown lentils
- ½ cup rice
- 5-6 cups water
- 1 onion, chopped
- ¾ teaspoon salt
- ½ teaspoon cinnamon
- 4 ½ teaspoons olive oil
- 1 tablespoon ground cumin

DIRECTIONS

1. Pour the olive oil into the crock pot. Turn the pot to the highest and add the chopped onion. Let the onions warm in the oil for 10-15 minutes.
2. Pour in the water (start with 5 cups, if necessary, add the remaining cup of water later) and the remaining ingredients.
3. Cover the pot and cook for 8 hours on low or 4-5 hours on high, stirring occasionally. If it is dry, pour in a little water, but not too much.
4. Serve warm.

Nutrition: Calories: 336; Carbohydrates 121 g; Protein 19 g; Fat 5 g; Sodium 578 mg

92. HAND-MADE RICE MILK

Preparation Time: 10 minutes   **Cooking Time:** 10 minutes   **Servings:** 2

INGREDIENTS

- 100 g cooked rice (white or brown)
- 500 ml water
- 1 teaspoon sugar
- Pinch salt

DIRECTIONS

1. Put all the ingredients and pour 1/3 of the water into a food processor.
2. Turn the food processor on and shred the rice into micro small pieces. Brown rice is harder than white rice so it takes longer to process the brown rice.
3. Pour the rest of the water into the food processor and mix further until you get a smooth milky looking texture.
4. Pour in a glass and serve.

Nutrition: Calories: 146; Carbohydrates 33 g; Protein 2 g; Fat 0 g

93. RICE CHEESE CHIPS

Preparation Time: 10 minutes   **Cooking Time:** 10 minutes   **Servings:** 6

INGREDIENTS

- 80 g cooked rice (white or brown)
- 1 tablespoon Parmesan cheese
- 1 tablespoon almond powder
- 1 tablespoon dry parsley
- ¼ teaspoon salt

DIRECTIONS

1. Warm up the cooked rice in a microwave wave if it's cold.
2. Put the rice and the rest of the ingredients in a plastic bag and mash the rice with your hands to get a cookie dough-like texture.
3. Divide the rice dough into bite-sized pieces and roll it up to make small rice balls.
4. Put the rice balls on a cooking sheet and cover them with plastic wrap.
5. Flatten the rice balls over the wrap to make rice chips.
6. Take off the wrap and put the rice chips into a microwave. Heat them to dry off water for about 5 minutes at 600 watts.
7. Take out the rice chips from the microwave and cool them at room temperature until it has set.
8. Serve on a plate.

Nutrition: Calories: 198; Carbohydrates 46 g; Protein 23 g; Fat 9 g; Fiber: 09 g

94. RICE MICROWAVE STEAM CAKE

Preparation Time: 10 minutes   **Cooking Time:** 10 minutes   **Servings:** 4

INGREDIENTS

- 1 tablespoon sweet rice flour
- 200 g cooked sweet potato
- 3 tablespoons coconut milk
- 3 teaspoons cinnamon powder

DIRECTIONS

1. Add the rice flour and sugar with the coconut milk. Mix well and make sure all the crumbs of rice flour become smooth and incorporate them with the other ingredients.
2. Mash the sweet potato.
3. Add the sweet potato with the rest of the filling. Mix well until you get a smooth texture.
4. Layout a plastic wrap and put the sweet potato filling.
5. Wrap up and roll up the sweet potato filling.
6. Heat the sweet potato roll in a microwave for about 3-4 minutes.
7. Cool the sweet potato roll at room temperature and cut the roll into individual pieces.
8. Serve on a plate.

Nutrition: Calories: 248; Carbohydrates 38 g; Protein 5 g; Fat 11 g

95. RICE NON-BAKE COCONUT PUDDING

Preparation Time: 10 minutes   **Cooking Time:** 30 minutes   **Servings:** 4

INGREDIENTS

- 100 g cooked rice
- 450 ml coconut milk
- 2 tablespoons sugar
- Cinnamon to taste, for topping

DIRECTIONS

1. Put all the ingredients except the cinnamon in a food processor and grind them until you get a smooth texture.
2. Put the rice cream in a pan and turn to low heat.
3. Cook down the rice cream until it becomes thick.
4. Cool the rice cream at room temperature.
5. Pour the rice cream into cups and cool them in a refrigerator for about 1 hour.
6. Sprinkle the cinnamon powder on top and serve.

Nutrition: Calories: 287; Fat 11 g; Carbohydrates 36 g; Protein 16 g; Fiber: 3.4 g

96. CARAMEL POP RICE

Preparation Time: 10 minutes   **Cooking Time:** 30 minutes   **Servings:** 4

INGREDIENTS

- 150 g rice (white or brown)
- 4 tablespoons sugar
- 1 tablespoon butter
- 2 tablespoons milk

DIRECTIONS

1. Rinse the rice with water as instructed on your rice package.
2. Put the rice in a frying pan and roast the rice at high heat until the rice starts to pop.
3. Turn to medium heat and cover the frying pan with a lid. Roast the rice for about 5-8 minutes until it turns brown.
4. Take out the rice from the pan.
5. Put the sugar, butter, and milk in the flying pan and bring it to a boil at high heat.
6. Put back the rice in the pan and cook them down until it becomes thick.
7. Spread the rice over a cooking sheet and cool it to room temperature.
8. Break the rice into bite-sized pieces and serve.

Nutrition: Calories: 169; Carbohydrates 357 g; Protein 12 g; Fat 8 g

97. RICE PUDDING

Preparation Time: 10 minutes   **Cooking Time:** 10 minutes   **Servings:** 2

INGREDIENTS

- 100 g cooked rice
- 300 ml milk
- 50 ml heavy cream
- 1 ¼ tablespoon sugar
- 1 egg yolk
- 1 tablespoon raisins
- 1 tablespoon sliced almond
- ¼ teaspoon vanilla extract
- Cinnamon and nutmeg, to taste

DIRECTIONS

1. Put the milk, sugar, and spices in a pan and turn to low heat. Stir gently until all the ingredients melt.
2. Add the cooked rice to the pan and cook down the rice cream until it becomes thick.
3. Turn off the heat and cool the rice cream to room temperature.
4. Add the heavy cream, egg yolk, raisins, and almonds to the rice cream. Mix thoroughly.
5. Pour the rice cream into an oven-proof container and bake them in an oven at 170°C or 340°F for about 8-10 minutes until lightly browned.
6. Cool down the pudding at room temperature and serve.

Nutrition: Calories: 567; Carbohydrates 46 g; Protein 16 g; Fat 37g; Fiber: 26.9 g

CHAPTER 5
DAILY BEANS RECIPES

98. NAVY DRY BEANS

Preparation Time: 5 minutes   **Cooking Time:** 35 minutes   **Servings:** 3

INGREDIENTS

- 1 pound navy beans
- 4 cups water
- 5 cups vinegar
- 1 cup lemon juice

DIRECTIONS

1. Remove any foreign objects from the beans, then add them to a bowl with water until covered.
2. Add vinegar and lemon juice to the soaking water and soak overnight.
3. Wash the beans and drain them. Transfer them to a large pot.
4. Cover with 2 inches of water. Bring the beans to a boil and frequently stir them.
5. Add the beans into your jars, preserving the cooking liquid and leaving 1-inch headspace.
6. Add the cooking liquid to the jars maintaining the 1-inch headspace.
7. Clean the rims and place the lids and the rings on the jars.
8. Transfer the jars into a pressure canner and process them at 10 pounds for 1 hour and 15 minutes.
9. Let the canner depressurize to zero before removing the jars. Let all cool and check the lids if they are properly sealed.
10. Store the jars.

Nutrition: Calories: 647; Carbohydrates 98 g; Protein 21 g; Fat 5 g; Fiber: 20 g; Sodium 489 mg

99. VEGETARIAN EXPRESS CHILI

Preparation Time: 10 minutes   **Cooking Time:** 10 minutes   **Servings:** 4

INGREDIENTS

- 1 can black beans, drained
- 1 can red kidney beans, drained
- 1 can pinto beans, drained
- 1 can crushed tomatoes
- 2 medium size white onions, chopped
- 3 large garlic cloves, chopped
- 1 cup water
- 5 tablespoon olive oil
- 1 tablespoon chili powder
- 1 tablespoon cumin powder
- ½ teaspoon chipotle chili powder
- Pinch cinnamon
- Salt and pepper

DIRECTIONS

1. Sauté onions and garlic in oil for around 5 minutes.
2. Mix chili powder and cumin powder, then cook for 1 minute Add crushed tomatoes and bring to a simmer.
3. Add beans, water, chipotle chili powder, and a pinch of cinnamon. Bring to a boil and simmer uncovered. Stir occasionally.
4. When the sauce thickens, season with salt and pepper before serving.

Nutrition: Calories: 1109; Carbohydrates 228 g; Protein 48 g; Fat 10 g; Sodium 110 mg

100. PERFECT MORNING BEAN EGGS

Preparation Time: 15 minutes   **Cooking Time:** 25 minutes   **Servings:** 2

INGREDIENTS

- 2 tablespoons unsalted butter
- 2 medium garlic cloves, finely chopped
- 1 medium onion, finely chopped
- 2 tablespoons light brown sugar
- 2 (15.5 ounces) cans cannellini beans, drained and rinsed; or 5 ounces dry cannellini beans, soaked and cooked
- ½ cup ketchup
- 2 teaspoons Worcestershire sauce
- ½ cup water
- Freshly ground black pepper and kosher salt, to taste
- 1 tablespoon olive oil
- 4 large eggs
- 4 slices bread, toasted

DIRECTIONS

1. In a medium saucepan or skillet, heat the butter over medium heat until melted.
2. Add the onion and garlic. Cook until softened, about 3-4 minutes.
3. Mix in the brown sugar, beans, ketchup, Worcestershire sauce, and water. Simmer for 5 minutes or until the mixture thickens.
4. Season to taste with freshly ground black pepper and salt, then remove from heat.
5. In another medium saucepan or skillet, heat oil over medium heat.
6. Crack the eggs, adding more pepper and salt to taste. Cook until yolks are runny, and whites are set.
7. Over the toasted bread, add the bean mixture and top with the eggs.
8. Serve warm.

Nutrition: Calories: 987; Carbohydrates 156 g; Protein 27 g; Fat 21g; Sodium 701 mg

101. SWEET POTATO BEAN BREAKFAST BOWL

Preparation Time: 15 minutes   **Cooking Time:** 15 minutes   **Servings:** 4

INGREDIENTS

- 4 tablespoons olive oil
- ½ yellow onion, diced
- 1 red bell pepper, cored and sliced
- 3 cups sweet potato, diced
- Freshly ground black pepper and kosher salt, to taste
- ½ tablespoon paprika
- 1 teaspoon ground cumin
- 2 cups spinach, torn into small pieces
- 1 (15 ounces) can black beans, drained and rinsed; or 5 ounces dry black beans, soaked and cooked

DIRECTIONS

1. In a medium saucepan, heat oil over medium heat.
2. Add the bell pepper, onion, and sweet potato, then season with freshly ground black pepper and salt.
3. Place the ground cumin and paprika. Cook until softened, about 8-10 minutes.
4. Add the spinach and cook until wilted, about 4-5 minutes.
5. Pour the beans and combine well.
6. Serve the beans with the toppings of your choice (sliced avocado, cooked eggs, toast, etc.)

Nutrition: Calories: 1112; Carbohydrates 250 g; Protein 48 g; Fat 28 g; Sodium 287 mg

102. BLACK BEAN OMELET

Preparation Time: 15 minutes   **Cooking Time:** 25 minutes   **Servings:** 2

INGREDIENTS

- 1 lime, juiced
- ¼ teaspoon ground cumin
- 1 (14-16 ounces) can black beans, drained and rinsed
- Hot sauce, to taste
- 1 tablespoon olive oil or butter
- 8 large eggs
- Freshly ground black pepper and salt, to taste
- ½ cup feta cheese, divided, plus more for serving
- Pico de gallo or bottled/canned salsa
- 1 avocado, pitted and sliced (optional)

DIRECTIONS

1. In a blender or food processor, mix the lime juice, ground cumin, beans, and hot sauce. Pulse until you get the consistency of refried beans. Add some water if the mixture is too thick.
2. In a medium saucepan or skillet, heat oil or butter over medium heat.
3. Crack two eggs into the pan. Using a spatula, stir gently to make a circle. Cook over one side, flip, then cook the other side. Cook until the eggs are well-set.
4. Add ¼ of the beans mixture and 2 tablespoons of the feta cheese in the center, then fold the omelet to cover the bean mixture.
5. Set aside on a serving plate.
6. Repeat the same process to make another omelet using the remaining ingredients.
7. Serve warm.

Nutrition: Calories: 985; Carbohydrates 78 g; Protein 77 g; Fat 38 g; Sodium 480 mg

103. LENTIL STUFFED PEPPERS

Preparation Time: 10 minutes   **Cooking Time:** 30 minutes   **Servings:** 4

INGREDIENTS

- 6 green bell peppers
- 1 pound ground beef
- 1 onion, chopped
- 1 red bell pepper, chopped
- 6 garlic cloves, minced
- 14 ounces mild salsa
- 2 ½ cups cooked lentils
- 1 cup grated cheddar cheese

DIRECTIONS

1. Preheat your oven to 375°F.
2. Cut the peppers in half lengthwise, and scoop out the seeds and pulp inside. Lay them out on a baking dish and set aside.
3. Place a pan over medium heat and add the olive oil.
4. Cook the garlic, red pepper, and onion in the oil for 2 minutes then add the ground beef.
5. Ensure everything is well mixed and cook for 10 minutes, make sure the mince is browned all over.
6. Add the salsa, mix well, and warm for 1 minute.
7. Take off the heat and add the lentils. Fold everything together to mix.
8. Spoon the lentil and beef mixture into the pepper halves. If you have any leftovers just spoon them into the baking dish around the peppers. Sprinkle cheese over everything.
9. Bake in the oven for 20-25 minutes.

Nutrition: Calories: 1890; Carbohydrates 169 g; Protein 162 g; Fat 68 g

104. LENTIL AND SPINACH STEW

Preparation Time: 10 minutes   **Cooking Time:** 30 minutes   **Servings:** 4

INGREDIENTS

- 1 tablespoon olive oil
- 3 onions, roughly chopped into large pieces
- 3 garlic cloves, minced
- ½ cup dried lentils
- 2 cups water
- 10 ounces frozen spinach
- 2 teaspoons ground cumin
- Sea salt and ground black pepper, to taste
- 2 garlic cloves, crushed

DIRECTIONS

1. Place a pan over medium heat and add the oil.
2. Cook the onion for 4 minutes then add the garlic. Stir well and cook for a further 5 minutes.
3. Add the lentils and water to the pan, then mix well. Bring to a boil, reduce heat, then cover and let simmer for 30-35 minutes. If you want the lentils to be tender, take off the heat at this point.
4. Defrost the spinach in the microwave and then add it to the lentils. Fold everything together.
5. Season with salt, pepper, and cumin. Mix well. Return to low heat and cook for 5 minutes, stirring occasionally.
6. Add the crushed garlic over the top, then season with salt and pepper before serving.

Nutrition: Calories: 765; Carbohydrates 86 g; Protein 23 g; Fat 19 g

105. PINTO BEAN AND HAM BAKE

Preparation Time: 10 minutes   **Cooking Time:** 30 minutes   **Servings:** 4

INGREDIENTS

- 2 cups pinto beans, dried
- 2 tablespoons bacon drippings
- 1 onion, chopped
- 1 green bell pepper, chopped
- 12 ounces chopped cooked ham
- ½ cup ketchup
- ¼ cup molasses
- 1 tablespoon vinegar
- 2 teaspoons Worcestershire sauce
- 1 ½ teaspoon dried mustard
- ½ cup reserved liquid (cooked beans)
- Sea salt, to taste

DIRECTIONS

1. Cook the pinto beans in a pot of boiling water until tender, around 30-40 minutes. Drain the beans and set aside. Be sure to reserve ½ cup of the water they were cooked in.
2. Preheat your oven to 325°F.
3. Place a pan over medium heat and add the bacon drippings. Cook for 30 seconds, then add the onion and pepper. Cook for 4-5 minutes, stirring frequently.
4. Take a casserole dish and create a base layer with the pinto beans. Add the onion and pepper mixture evenly over the top.
5. Create the next layer with the chopped ham. Sprinkle in the sea salt, to taste.
6. Mix all the remaining ingredients in a bowl, then pour evenly over the casserole dish.
7. Bake in the oven for 60 minutes.

Nutrition: Calories: 1127; Carbohydrates 121 g; Protein 37 g; Fat 45 g

106. BEAN QUESADILLAS

Preparation Time: 10 minutes   **Cooking Time:** 30 minutes   **Servings:** 4

INGREDIENTS

- ½ onion, finely chopped
- 2 garlic cloves, minced
- 1 can black beans, rinsed and drained
- 1 courgette, chopped
- 1 teaspoon ground cayenne
- 1 teaspoon red chili flakes
- ½ green bell pepper, chopped
- 2 large tomatoes, chopped
- 4 (12 inches) flour tortillas
- ⅓ cup shredded cheddar cheese
- 2 tablespoons olive oil

DIRECTIONS

1. Place a pan over medium heat and add 1 tablespoon of olive oil.
2. Cook the garlic and onion in the oil for 4-5 minutes.
3. Add the pepper, beans, chopped tomatoes, courgette, and chili flakes. Cook for 4-6 minutes, stirring frequently.
4. Place a new pan over medium heat and add ½ tablespoon of olive oil. Add 1 tortilla to the pan and then spoon half of the bean mixture onto it. Sprinkle with ½ of the cheese and then lay another tortilla over it.
5. Cook for 1-2 minutes, then carefully flip the quesadilla and repeat.
6. Repeat with the remaining tortillas and the bean mixture.
7. Cut the quesadillas into wedges before serving.

Nutrition: Calories: 1294; Carbohydrates 185 g; Protein 60 g; Fat 36 g

107. SOUTHERN PORK AND CANNELLINI BEANS

Preparation Time: 15 minutes   **Cooking Time:** 30 minutes   **Servings:** 2

INGREDIENTS

- 1 yellow onion, sliced
- 5 ½ ounces gammon steak, fat trimmed and cut into bite-sized pieces
- 9 ounces pork tenderloin fillet, fat trimmed and cut into bite-sized pieces
- 2 garlic cloves, crushed
- 2 teaspoons smoked paprika
- ½ teaspoon hot chili powder
- 2 (14 ounces) cans cannellini beans, drained and rinsed; or 10 ounces dry cannellini beans, soaked and cooked
- 1 (14 ounces) can chopped tomatoes with their juices
- 2 tablespoons tomato purée
- 2 teaspoons prepared English mustard
- 1 ¾ cup low-sodium pork or chicken stock
- 3 heaped tablespoons flat-leaf parsley, chopped and divided
- 4 tablespoons low-fat plain yogurt
- Freshly ground black pepper and kosher salt, to taste

DIRECTIONS

1. Spray a medium saucepan or skillet with cooking oil. Heat over medium heat.
2. Add the onion and cook until softened and translucent, about 4-5 minutes.
3. Season the gammon and pork with freshly ground black pepper. Add to the skillet and cook for 2 minutes.
4. Add the garlic, chili powder, and paprika, then cook for a few seconds.
5. Place the beans, tomato puree, mustard, and tomatoes. Pour the stock and stir gently, then bring to a simmer.
6. Cook until the pork is cooked through, and the mixture thickens about 20-25 minutes.
7. Add half the chopped parsley and stir.
8. Serve warm with the remaining parsley on top along with a dollop of yogurt.

Nutrition: Calories: 1936; Carbohydrates 136 g; Protein 54 g; Fat 54 g; Sodium 364 mg

108. CLASSIC BLACK BEAN CHILI

Preparation Time: 10 minutes   **Cooking Time:** 30 minutes   **Servings:** 4

INGREDIENTS

- ¼ cup olive oil
- 2 medium red bell peppers, cored and coarsely chopped
- 2 cups yellow onion, chopped
- 6 garlic cloves, chopped
- 2 teaspoons dried oregano
- 2 tablespoons chili powder
- 1½ teaspoons ground cumin
- ½ teaspoon cayenne pepper
- 3 (15 ounces) cans black beans, drained (but reserve ½ cup of the bean liquid); or 5 ounces dry black beans, soaked and cooked
- 1 (16 ounces) can tomato sauce

For Garnish:

- Sour cream, grated Monterey Jack cheese, chopped cilantro, and chopped green onion.

DIRECTIONS

1. In a medium to large stockpot/deep saucepan/Dutch oven, heat oil over medium heat.
2. Add the bell peppers, garlic, and onion. Cook until softened and translucent, about 8-10 minutes.
3. Add the oregano, chili powder, ground cumin, and cayenne pepper. Cook for 2 minutes.
4. Add the tomato sauce, beans, and reserved bean liquid. Bring to a boil.
5. Over medium-low heat, simmer the mixture for about 15 minutes.
6. Season to taste with freshly ground black pepper and kosher salt.
7. Divide the chili into serving bowls. Top with sour cream, grated cheese, chopped cilantro, and chopped green onion.
8. Serve warm.

Nutrition: Calories: 876; Carbohydrates 143 g; Protein 52 g; Fat 34 g; Sodium 736 mg

109. BLACK BEAN MUSHROOM FETTUCCINE

Preparation Time: 10 minutes   **Cooking Time:** 30 minutes   **Servings:** 4

INGREDIENTS

- 9 ounces whole-wheat fettuccine
- 1 tablespoon olive oil
- ¾ cups baby Portobello mushrooms, sliced
- 1 garlic clove, minced
- 1 (14.5 ounces) can diced tomatoes with their juices
- 1 (15 ounces) can black beans, drained and rinsed; or 5 ounces dry black beans, soaked and cooked
- 1 teaspoon dried rosemary
- ½ teaspoon dried oregano
- 2 cups baby spinach

DIRECTIONS

1. Cook pasta according to package directions in boiling water. Drain and set aside.
2. In a large skillet, heat oil over medium heat.
3. Add the mushrooms and cook until tender, about 4-6 minutes.
4. Place the garlic and cook until fragrant, about 1 minute.
5. Add the tomatoes, beans, rosemary, and oregano. Cook until evenly heated, about 1 minute.
6. Mix the spinach and cook until wilted, about 2 minutes.
7. Add the cooked pasta and toss to combine well.
8. Serve warm.

Nutrition: Calories: 1472; Carbohydrates 283 g; Protein 76 g; Fat 6 g; Sodium 230 mg

110. WHITE BEAN SHRIMP SPAGHETTI

Preparation Time: 10 minutes   **Cooking Time:** 30 minutes   **Servings:** 4

INGREDIENTS

- 8 ounces whole-wheat spaghetti
- Kosher salt, to taste
- Freshly ground black pepper, to taste
- ¼ cup extra-virgin olive oil
- 1 shallot, chopped
- 1 (14 ounces) can white beans, drained and rinsed; or 5 ounces dry white beans, soaked and cooked
- 3 jarred cherry peppers or pepperoncini, roughly chopped
- 2 garlic cloves, chopped
- ¼-½ teaspoon crushed red pepper flakes
- ¾ pound medium shrimp, peeled and deveined
- ½ cup dry white wine
- ½ lemon, juiced and zested
- ½ cup flat-leaf parsley, roughly chopped

DIRECTIONS

1. Cook pasta according to package directions in boiling water. Reserve ⅔ cup of the pasta water, then drain and set aside.
2. In a medium saucepan or skillet, heat oil over medium heat.
3. Add the shallot and cook until softened and translucent, about 2 minutes.
4. Stir the cherry peppers/pepperoncini, beans, garlic, crushed red pepper flakes, and ½ teaspoon of kosher salt. Continue to cook until garlic is mildly browned, about 2-3 minutes.
5. Mix in the shrimp and cook for 3 minutes or until opaque.
6. Pour the wine and cook for 2 minutes.
7. Add the lemon zest and pasta. Toss to combine well.
8. Pour the pasta water, freshly ground black pepper, kosher salt, and parsley.
9. Stir gently and serve warm.

Nutrition: Calories: 1876; Carbohydrates 198 g; Protein 48 g; Fat 11 g; Sodium 914 mg

111. PARMESAN TUSCAN BEAN PASTA

Preparation Time: 10 minutes   **Cooking Time:** 30 minutes   **Servings:** 4

INGREDIENTS

- 8 ounces linguine or fettuccine pasta
- 1 tablespoon olive oil
- 1 tablespoon unsalted butter
- 3 garlic cloves, minced
- 1 pint cherry or grape tomatoes
- 10 cranks freshly ground black pepper
- ½ teaspoon kosher salt
- ½ teaspoon dried basil
- 1 (15 ounces) can cannellini beans, drained and rinsed; or 5 ounces dry cannellini beans, soaked and cooked
- 4 ounces baby spinach
- 3 ounces parmesan cheese, shredded

DIRECTIONS

1. Cook pasta according to package directions in boiling water. Drain and set aside.
2. In a large skillet, heat butter and olive oil over medium heat.
3. Add the garlic and cook until fragrant, about one minute.
4. Mix the tomatoes, freshly ground black pepper, kosher salt, and basil. Cook until tomatoes start to release their juices and their skin bursts.
5. Mix in the spinach and cook until wilted, about 2 minutes.
6. Pour the beans and cook until heated for about 2 minutes.
7. Add more kosher salt to taste, then add the pasta and stir to coat evenly with the pan sauce.
8. Top with the shredded parmesan and serve warm.

Nutrition: Calories: 1032, 29 g; Carbohydrates 161 g; Protein 52 g; Sodium 1134 mg

112. ANCHOVY WHITE BEAN PASTA

Preparation Time: 10 minutes   **Cooking Time:** 30 minutes   **Servings:** 4

INGREDIENTS

- 4 tablespoons olive oil
- 4 medium garlic cloves, minced
- 4 anchovy fillets, minced
- 1 teaspoon crushed red pepper flakes
- 2 (15.5 ounces) cans white beans or cannellini beans, drained and rinsed; or 10 ounces dry white/cannellini beans, soaked and cooked
- 1 ⅓ cup low-sodium vegetable stock
- 1 splash heavy cream (optional)
- Pinch freshly ground black pepper and kosher salt, or to taste
- 1 pound orecchiette, penne, or tubular pasta of your choice
- 1 ½ pound broccoli rabe, trimmed and cut into 1½-inch pieces
- ½ lemon, juiced
- ½ cup ricotta cheese (optional)
- ½ cup parmesan cheese, grated (optional)

DIRECTIONS

1. In a medium saucepan or skillet, heat oil over medium-low heat.
2. Add the garlic, anchovy fillets, and crushed red pepper flakes. Cook until anchovies dissolve, about 1-2 minutes.
3. Add the stock, beans, and heavy cream (if using).
4. Simmer for 4-5 minutes or until the mixture thickens. Gently smash the beans (do not break them) to make them half-mushy.
5. Remove from the heat, then season with freshly ground black pepper and kosher salt, to taste.
6. Cook the pasta per package directions in boiling water. Reserve ⅓ cup of the pasta water, then drain and set aside.
7. In boiling water, cook the broccoli rabe until wilted, about 3-4 minutes. Drain and set aside.
8. In a large deep saucepan, add the broccoli rabe, pasta, and reserved pasta water. Simmer for 1 minute over low heat.
9. Season to taste with freshly ground black pepper and kosher salt. Mix in the lemon juice and a few dollops of ricotta cheese, if desired.
10. Top with the parmesan cheese and crushed red pepper flakes, then serve.

Nutrition: Calories: 2386; Carbohydrates 563 g; Protein 190 g; Fat 30 g; Sodium 1528 mg

113. BROCCOLI NAVY BEAN PASTA

Preparation Time: 10 minutes   **Cooking Time:** 30 minutes   **Servings:** 4

INGREDIENTS

- 1 pound whole-wheat spaghetti
- 12 garlic cloves, peeled and thinly sliced
- 3 cups canned navy beans, drained and rinsed; or 1 cup dry navy beans, soaked and cooked
- 1 broccoli head, cut into slim florets
- 1 medium onion, sliced
- 1 lemon, juiced
- 1 teaspoon crushed red pepper flakes
- Freshly ground black pepper and kosher salt, to taste
- 1 tablespoon extra-virgin olive oil
- 1 packed cup flat-leaf parsley, minced

DIRECTIONS

1. Cook pasta according to package directions in boiling water. Drain water and set cooked pasta aside, reserving ½ cup of the pasta water.
2. In a medium saucepan or skillet, heat oil over medium heat.
3. Add the onion, garlic, freshly ground black pepper, and kosher salt. Cook until onion is softened and translucent, about 7-8 minutes.
4. Mix the crushed red pepper flakes and broccoli florets. Cook for 5 minutes or until broccoli becomes slightly tender.
5. Pour the pasta, freshly ground black pepper, and kosher salt to taste. Add the reserved pasta water and stir to combine.
6. Add the lemon juice and parsley, then serve warm.

Nutrition: Calories: 1237; Carbohydrates 259 g; Protein 46 g; Fat 53 g; Sodium 257 mg

Desserts Beans Recipes

114. CRISPY CHICKPEAS

Preparation Time: 7 minutes   **Cooking Time:** 55 minutes   **Servings:** 4

INGREDIENTS

- 1 can chickpeas, drained
- 4 tablespoons olive oil
- Salt to taste
- Preferred seasoning

DIRECTIONS

1. Dry beans completely and lay them out on a baking sheet.
2. Drizzle olive oil and salt on the beans. Make sure all beans are covered in oil.
3. Bake for 30 minutes at 400°F until golden brown and crunchy.
4. Toss in seasoning before serving.

Nutrition: Calories: 871; Carbohydrates 60 g; Protein 23 g; Fat 63 g; Sodium 217 mg

115. SPICY CHICKPEAS

Preparation Time: 7 minutes   **Cooking Time:** 43 minutes   **Servings:** 4

INGREDIENTS

- 1 can chickpeas, drained
- 4 tablespoons olive oil
- 1 teaspoon cumin
- 1 teaspoon chili powder
- 1 teaspoon cayenne pepper
- ½ teaspoon sea salt

DIRECTIONS

1. Dry beans completely and lay them out on a baking sheet.
2. Drizzle olive oil and spices on the beans. Make sure all beans are covered in oil.
3. Bake for 30 minutes at 400°F until golden brown and crunchy.
4. Season with salt before serving.

Nutrition: Calories: 882; Carbohydrates 65 g; Protein 23 g; Fat 63 g; Sodium 950 mg

116. WHITE BEAN DIP

Preparation Time: 7 minutes   **Cooking Time:** 33 minutes   **Servings:** 4

INGREDIENTS

- 1 can cannellini beans, drained
- 5 tablespoons olive oil
- 3 garlic cloves, minced
- 2 tablespoon lime juice
- ¼ cup fresh parsley, chopped
- Pita bread
- Salt and pepper, to taste

DIRECTIONS

1. Place beans, garlic, olive oil, lime juice, and parsley in a food processor.
2. Puree until smooth.
3. Season with salt and pepper before serving with warm pita bread.

Nutrition: Calories: 987; Carbohydrates 169 g; Protein 21 g; Fat 16 g; Sugar 5 g; Sodium 418 mg

117. CHAMPION BEAN DIP

Preparation Time: 7 minutes   **Cooking Time:** 55 minutes   **Servings:** 4

INGREDIENTS

- 1 can pinto beans, drained
- 1 cup cheddar cheese, grated
- 1 cup sour cream
- 1 package cream cheese, softened
- ½ teaspoon cumin
- 1/2 teaspoon chili powder
- ½ teaspoon cayenne
- 100 g tortilla chips (or as required)

DIRECTIONS

1. In a large bowl, mash beans.
2. Add all ingredients except for the tortilla chips and heat in the microwave until the beans are heated through.
3. Serve with tortilla chips.

Nutrition: Calories: 1591; Carbohydrates 160 g; Protein 69 g; Fat 82 g; Sodium 92 mg

CONCLUSION

Yes, if you know how to use your beans and grains to their best capacity. Beans and rice are high in energy, nutrients, vitamins, and minerals. And they can be used in many ways than just "beans and rice."

Could you imagine eating nothing but beans and rice every day? Food fatigue would set very rapidly. In a survival crisis, which would be disastrous for any survivalist. However, if you know how to vary the flavor and produce a variety of recipes with these energy ingredients, your stock of beans and rice will be the most precious asset in your cabinet. Beans and rice are wonderful foods to stockpile since they store well and last a long time. The legumes will keep in their original packaging for 1-2 years if bugs or rodents do not get to them. Use the freshest beans you can get for the greatest outcomes. For short-term storage, they can also be stored in plastic, glass, or metal containers.

Beans are a great addition to your regular meal preparation. Aside from the health benefits, beans can be used to make a variety of dishes for a low cost. They are simple to prepare if you use canned ones. Simply heat for a few minutes, then add a few more ingredients to make a flavorful meal. You can also substitute the beans for meat in your recipes. You save money on food and are probably healthier as a result.

Beans come in a variety of shapes, sizes, and colors, but their nutritional advantages are strikingly similar. So, whether you consume pinto beans, cranberry beans, lentils, baby limas, black beans, white beans, chickpeas, or charming little black-eyed peas, you and your family are getting the twelve vital nutrients contained in beans. They may help prevent colon cancer and other malignancies, as well as heart disease, excessive cholesterol, and digestive problems. They include a lot of vitamins and minerals, which have been linked to more energy and vitality. These seeds are also great for keeping blood sugar levels in check. Beans contain a lot of fiber and protein. They will fill you up and slow your digestion, keeping you from feeling starved while on a diet.

ENJOY!!!

Made in the USA
Las Vegas, NV
17 July 2023

74880553R00050